Conversations with a Tree

Rashana

This book is dedicated to all who have
the courage to step out of
the busyness of life and back into
the stillness of nature.

ISBN 978-0-9920307-8-0 (Paperback)
ISBN 978-0-9920307-9-7 (ebook)
Available on Amazon

Published in Canada by
Inner Nature Publishing
PO Box 208
Bear River, NS
B0S 1B0

Table of Contents

Preface

Trees are sanctuaries. Whoever knows how to speak to them, whoever knows how to listen to them, can learn the truth. They do not preach learning and precepts, they preach, undeterred by particulars, the ancient law of life. *~ Herman Hesse ~*

Every January 6th I celebrate my birthday which, in itself, is nothing extraordinary. Being middle aged, I have done that many times. And yet, what I came to realize in 2012, was that a birthday so early in the year is like a double beginning. There are all the changes and resolutions that we think about when a new calendar year approaches as well as the changing energy and numerology that a new personal year brings. Add to that my determination that 2012 was going to be a year of healing and you have a formula for change! I was ready for life to be full and rich and I knew that the only way to get there was to come face to face with my wounds. At the time I was living in a small city working at a job that just did not resonate with who I am. Every day I prayed to be out of there, and the universe provided. On January 23rd I arrived at work at 8:30 and was gone by 9:00! I'll never forget it. It was the first day of the Chinese Year of the Dragon – another new beginning! I was 'released' from the job that I hated. Of course I was surprised at this totally unexpected turn of events but I connected with the blessing of it almost immediately. I went home and did my happy dance, knowing that my prayers had been answered even though the outcome was definitely not what I had expected.

I was proud of the way I handled that experience. My new mantra was 'all change leads to something better' and I was doing a good job of trusting that. Then, about six weeks after losing my job, I learned that my landlord was selling the condo I was living in and I had to move. My mind immediately went into the past directly to fear. It brought up an experience, just two years earlier, of big challenges that happened in January. On the day of my birthday, my roommate at the time announced he was moving out the end of the month leaving me responsible for all the household expenses and the rent. It was more than my income would cover! There was no written contract. Then, a week later, someone ran into my car while I was sitting in rush hour traffic. It was a write-off. My most recent news immediately took me back to what seemed to be a pattern of events around my birthday, and the fear of how I would get through this. But just as quickly it changed. This time I was determined to stay in a place of trust instead of dropping into the 'why me?' Fully confident that Spirit was providing opportunities and not hardship, I realized that with no job holding me in the city, and the need to move, I was free to live wherever I wanted.

It is so interesting the way things work. Just two days before my notification of the move, I had the thought that I wanted to live out of the city and be more connected to nature. As well, I had already done some healing work around my relationships with family. Both those factors influenced my decision to move to a nearby town that I had always loved. I would be closer to nature and closer to family. By June 1st I was moving into my new apartment and, for the first time in my life I felt like I was truly home. I spent the summer in total bliss because of the beauty of my surroundings. I had trees and birds outside my window and one of the most beautiful views I have ever seen from the main street of town.

As I began to explore this little town I discovered a trail that goes through some woods with a little stream running by. At one point there is a pond with a small bridge that crosses over the stream feeding out of the pond.

On the other side of the bridge the trail divides, passing on either side of a tall hemlock tree. One day I stopped to admire the tree. I put my hands on the bark and sat on one of the large roots at its base. And then I 'sensed' an invitation into conversation. As someone who is highly intuitive, when the tree 'spoke' to me, it was not much of a stretch for me to accept that this would be possible. I have always had the understanding that there is so much more potential to life than what the rational mind perceives.

And so I found myself at the base of a stately hemlock tree having a conversation! She told me she would like to be called Henrietta, after a young woman who used to sit at her base 100 years ago, lamenting lost loves. Henrietta asked me to buy a journal to record her wisdom and I have been visiting with her ever since. She feels like an old friend. It is incredible the love that I have felt from her. It has moved me to tears at times. I have also been moved to tears at the sight of sunlight streaming through the trees. I believe that we are more connected to our true self ~ our spirit ~ when we are in nature making it easier to access and feel the deep love that is the source of all creation.

I find great comfort in this connection with the natural world. It really is like heaven on earth for me.

When I am among the trees I am more present and I feel whole. As a teenager I would go to the woods to find a sanctuary away from my troubled life. As an adult I have been touched to the depth of my soul by the loving energy that comes with being among the trees. If you can be present with nature, fully immersed in its wonder, you will find it too. This book is an invitation into my new world – my something better.

Part I

~ Uncovering the Research ~

As one person who has experienced the indifference of many scientists in this field I can simply state that such a high resistance to new ideas does not concern me. I have a truly wonderful ally: Mother Nature. *~ Cleve Backster ~*

When I started sharing my tree messages I was a bit choosy about who I would tell. Of course, inevitably, I was going to run into some skepticism. I am not someone who needs proof outside of my own personal experience. I have always believed anecdotal evidence because I trust that people know what they are experiencing. However, it is easy to understand why others, who are not having the visceral experience that I am, would have trouble accepting what I was saying about being able to communicate with trees. For that reason I have decided to include this chapter to bring forward scientific studies revealing that the life of plants holds many more similarities to the animal kingdom than we have been led to believe. In this chapter I will touch on many different findings of the properties of plants and the benefits of nature and leave it to you to further study anything that interests you. My intention is to broaden the reader's understanding of the sensitive attributes of plants and 'plant a seed' of curiosity about the potential of a true connection between humans and plants and how indeed that would influence our treatment of the natural world and our role as protectors of this planet and all life upon it.

Once I started thinking of acquiring research around my ability to connect with trees, I stumbled upon a video on YouTube of a 1979 documentary called *The Secret Life of Plants.* The documentary is based on a book of the same name written in 1973 by Peter Tompkins and Christopher Bird. The book reveals remarkable discoveries about plants far beyond the acceptable wisdom that they have curative properties. The authors reveal that plants respond to music and the human voice as well as having the ability to communicate with people! What I find interesting is that some of the greatest proof of the sensitive nature of plants dates back to the 1970s. Being a baby boomer myself I can say that the 70s was a time of great spiritual awakening that somehow got stifled and dismissed. Instead of awakening to the potential of the natural world and our connection to it, we separated ourselves from it and now stand on the brink of the collapse of many of our ecosystems! A quick look at the dilemma of bees and the disappearing species of toads is proof of this. Both are like the canary in the mine, predicting perhaps that we are all about to falter.

The Secret Life of Plants speaks at length about one of the most inspirational researchers on the hidden attributes of plants - Cleve Backster. Backster started his career as a polygraph expert with the CIA and it was through his work with the polygraph that he discovered the 'awareness' of plants. Cleve Backster passed from this earthly plane in the summer of 2013 at the age of 89. He was a contemporary and yet his work is pretty much unknown. Backster dedicated his life to research on plants and never gave up trying to enlighten us on their amazing attributes despite much disregard from the rest of the scientific community. It is my hope that humanity is now ready to awaken to the potential that he and others have brought forward and to accept the connection and similarities of the plant and animal kingdoms.

Cleve Backster's work with plants started when he was sitting in his lab one day and decided to water his plant. He had the thought to hook the polygraph up to the plant to see if it showed a response to being watered. To his surprise, the plant showed a stressful response to the cold water. He then had the idea that he would burn the plant to see how it would respond to that. What happened then was quite incredible. The polygraph showed a stress response the moment he had the thought of burning the plant! He hadn't even gone to get the matches yet. The mere *thought* of harming the plant caused it to show a stress response! This started his research into the plant kingdom and brought forward proof that plants, like us, responded differently to positive and negative events.

Realizing that plants are capable of picking up on a person's thoughts, Backster started ensuring that his experiments were random so that his thoughts would not be affecting the plant's responses and influencing the results. In one experiment Backster placed a bowl of shrimp in water over a pot of boiling water. He had set up the experiment so that the bowl of shrimp, at a randomly selected time determined, would tip into the boiling water. In order not to influence the results by thinking about when the shrimp would drop into the boiling water, he programmed his computer to select the time and he left his office and went for a walk. When he returned, the polygraph showed that his plant reacted at the exact moment when the shrimp had been tipped into the boiling water. His plant was responding to the loss of life of the shrimp!

Further experiments by Backster showed a stress response in his plant when boiling water was poured down the sink drain. He assumed the plant responded because there were live bacteria in the drain that were being killed by the water. Another test showed that the live bacteria in yogurt showed stress when bacteria in chicken was being consumed by a cat. Backster's polygraph revealed incredible responses. Bear in mind that Cleve Backster was considered an expert in his field with the polygraph. It's not like he would be misinterpreting the readings.

Backster then started exploring beyond the reaction of plants. In one study he removed white blood cells from willing participants and attached the polygraph to the petri dishes that contained them. At the same time the participant, the donor of the white blood cells, was hooked up to another polygraph. He found that the white blood cells extracted from the donor would respond at the same time as the donor to emotional events such as looking at stimulating photos. In the case of a young male student looking at Playboy photos, the white blood cells went off the chart! When the magazine was closed the cells would calm down. When it was opened up again the cells' response would again be off the chart! This proved that our cells respond to our emotions even when removed from our bodies!

If, as Backster's studies have shown, plants have the ability to know our thoughts, is it such a stretch to think that we can do the same and know the thoughts of plants? Of course you know my answer to that. I believe that my ability to receive information from plants is related to my many years developing my abilities as a channel. In the beginning of my spiritual journey, almost twenty years ago, I had a great desire to be able to connect with what I call the Higher Beings of Light. From this it was not such a stretch for me to be able to perceive messages from trees. It is very exciting to discover that there is scientific proof of the sensitive nature of plants that is far beyond what most of us perceive as truth.

Another example of plant research is found in the book, *Blinded by Science* by Matthew Silverstone. The book brings together a variety of peer-reviewed scientific studies that have been all but hidden within our libraries without any recognition for their findings. It seems that these studies may not fit into what we like to consider the norm! Silverstone reveals findings from a book entitled *Your Inner Fish* written by Neil Schubin. Schubin again revealed that plants have very similar behavior to humans. Like us, plants apparently recognize their siblings and have the ability to communicate with them. Plants will produce less root mass when growing next to siblings as opposed to non-relative plants. This is an apparent interest in giving the young related plants good growing space. Remarkably, he also found that plants have memory. Plants that have been growing together will show a response when one of the plants is removed for several months and later returned to join the others. Like Backster, Schubin also found that plants are sensitive to harm caused to other plants. He found that trees in one stand or forest will respond when trees in another stand far away have been harmed.

In Chapter Seven of *Blinded by Science,* Silverstone introduces another pioneer who discovered the similarities between the plant and animal kingdom - J.C. Bose. Bose was a professor of science back in the late 1800s and early 1900s whose work was greatly dismissed by many in the scientific community. In *Blinded by Science* it is speculated that Bose's Indian ethnicity in a very British scientific community explains why his work was not well recognized. Bose's brilliance is evident. Even though he was the first to prove that radio waves could travel through the air and be collected at a different location, the invention of radio waves was credited to someone else two years later. Part of Bose's discoveries was that plant tissue and animal tissue show similar electrical response to a stimulus. Bose took this a step further showing that metals will also show a similar response to plants and animals, such as fatigue from being over-stimulated and even 'permanent irresponsiveness' which we would call death. According to Silverstone, Bose "determined that plants were behaviorally identical to animals." In fact, Bose showed that plants are actually more sensitive than us humans, being able to respond to wave lengths much shorter and much longer than our human capabilities. It is not my intention here to give in-depth results of these studies but to offer enough information to tweak your curiosity and perhaps lead you to your own research into these great discoveries.

What I find even more exciting than the research into the life of plants is research into the quantum field and all the implications of quantum physics. After having visited my tree friend Henrietta a few times I asked her how she could have so much wisdom to share being a tree after all! Her response was that she accesses the wisdom from the quantum 'field'. She added that humans have this ability as well but we have forgotten how to do it. She said that those who channel, like I do, access information from the field but simply are not aware of it. I found that to be a very interesting answer. A few days later I was on YouTube, watching a presentation by Gregg Braden – filmed in Italy in 2007 – and he said something that fascinated me. He told his audience that he had been invited to a scientist's lab where Einstein's brain was stored. Scientists had kept Einstein's brain thinking that, because of his intelligence, it might look different than most people's brains. It turns out there was no significant difference, but that is an aside. What Gregg Braden shared was that the scientists in this particular lab were researching the possibility that memory is not stored in the brain but that the brain is like an antennae that retrieves our memories from an external 'field'! I have to admit that this is very new research, but also very exciting, possibly confirming what Henrietta had said.

To bring you information about quantum research and all that it is revealing about the hidden aspects of life I turned to another fascinating YouTube video I had seen based on the book *The Holographic Universe.* In Part Two of the video it talks about the research of a brain scientist named Dr. Karl Lashley who, in the 1920s, found that "no matter what portion of a rat's brain he removed, he was

unable to eradicate its memory of how to perform complex tasks it had learned prior to surgery." Jump ahead almost 100 years and we find ourselves in the discoveries of the quantum field which may be able to make sense of Lashley's discovery. Quantum science likens our life experiences to a hologram. Dr. Karl Pribram, who is a neurosurgeon and neurophysiologist, also studies where memory is stored in the brain. Pribram set out to solve the mystery of Lashley's discovery with rats. In short, Pribram came to believe that memory does not travel through neurons but through "impulses of light that crisscross the entire brain" like a hologram. *The Holographic Universe* video states that Pribram believes "our brains mathematically construct 'hard' reality by relying on input from a frequency domain." (Michael Talbot, *The Holographic Universe)*. Pribram concludes that the brain's role is to receive waves from "a frequency domain" and interpret that information into the physical experience that we call life.
(https://www.youtube.com/watch?v=vU6yCD_sEvU).

Recent studies are also showing that the brain responds to imagination and what we call reality in the same way. Studies reveal the area of the brain that lights up when someone is having an actual experience also light up when the person is imagining the same experience. The same parts of the brain are activated. As a hypnotherapist I am aware that we can seemingly change reality through the subconscious which many would call the imagination. Someone who has stage fright can be released from that fear through hypnosis by going into the subconscious and changing the experience that created the fear in the first place. So what is real, the original experience or the released experience where the person being hypnotized is suddenly over their fear? I also have read that people with split personality disorder can have a diagnosed illness when presenting in one personality that does not appear in another personality. So, a person can, from one minute to the next, go from having a physical condition to not having it! If our bodies are solid reality how would this be possible? I believe quantum physics and the unfolding discoveries of 'the field' are the answer to that question.

In *The Holographic Universe* video they quote Pribram as saying "Your brain first receives a hologram in wave frequencies downloaded from the Field. It then translates those waves into particles to create your holographic "physical reality", and then it sends that "reality" "out there" for you to perceive and experience." What Pribram is saying is that our reality is like a hologram that the brain perceives and then projects “out there” for us to perceive as reality when it comes back to us! I can understand that it is hard to get your mind around this idea in the beginning. However, after a few years of playing with this concept it is making its way into a sense of comprehension for me so be patient with yourself if it interests you enough to give it more thought. (https://www.youtube.com/watch?v=vU6yCD_sEvU).

As I have said, my interest is not in proving the science around this or even getting into complicated explanations. I am much more experiential in my expression and less cerebral. However, I find the discoveries about plants and our perception of reality to be quite fascinating and a welcome bit of validation of my experiences with the natural world. That said I will end this chapter with some of the more experiential studies coming forward about our relationship with the natural world and how it impacts our wellbeing as humans.

There are studies starting to surface that are showing that children, including those with ADD, who are exposed to green spaces such as parks and wooded areas are calmer, more congenial, healthier and perform better academically. According to Silverstone in *Blinded by Science* it is the vibrational essence of nature that has the beneficial effects on humans. This would coincide with what Henrietta has said to me. I once was feeling quite out of sorts and so went to the wooded trail where Henrietta stands. I started to feel better immediately after entering the trail. When I got to Henrietta she told me that it was the love essence or vibration of the trees that made me feel better. It made sense to me, especially after she explained that I was picking up on a mass consciousness of fear and that was what had me feeling so uncomfortable. That being true, it would only make sense that I would feel better surrounded by trees that were emanating the vibration of love and not engaging in the fear.

In his book *Last Child in the Woods* Richard Louv reveals that natural surroundings support every aspect of children's development – physical, emotional, spiritual and mental. He found that children exposed to green space were more social with a greater willingness to share. Beyond the many studies that show health benefits and more happiness when in nature, Louv's work also shows an impact on one's values. Research showed that, when immersed in nature, participants placed the values of community and connection with others over wealth and fame.

In Asia doctors recommend walking in the forest and being in nature as an important aspect of maintaining health. The Korean Forest Research Institute has found that the chemicals from conifer trees are associated with positive health. In Korea it even has a name – forest bathing. Another term surfacing is 'earthing' which is simply walking in your bare feet on the grass or the earth. The fact that we have developed names for this connection back to nature speaks to me of how far removed we are from it. What in my childhood was simply referred to as walking bare foot now is called earthing and is considered a cure for many ailments such as stress and depression.

We are finding our way back to nature and a deeper connection with our earthly mother I am delighted to say. It may be slow but progress it is and research seems to be coming from around the world. Finnish studies show that time in nature reduces sick days and increases productivity. In Scotland, hospitals are being developed with more green space because they have found that patients recover faster when surrounded by plants. As I was in the process of putting this chapter together I woke up one morning and turned on the radio at my bedside. I found myself listening to the middle of an interview about outdoor preschools for four year old children. The particular school was located in a neighboring province to where I live in Canada and based on the work of Norwegian studies showing that children who have time outdoors get along better, share more, communicate more with each other and have better health.

There are many studies coming forward that speak of our connection to nature bringing us back to health. For me, the deepest and most profound benefit is our connection back to our true nature. I believe our spiritual self is connected to the natural world. When I am in nature I feel more myself and study participants have said the same thing. Yet most of humanity is lost in a world of technology and man-made structures and creations that have led us away from our nature as beings of love and joy. This book is an invitation back to our true nature. It is a world of peace and grace and most of all love. The love that I have felt from my dear tree friend Henrietta touches deep within my heart. There are no conditions, no needs, just love offered freely and felt deeply. I am delighted to be able to share her essence with you. May it lead you back – back to the truth of who you are in all your glory. Join me among the trees and the natural world and rediscover what is truly important in this world. It's not more stuff from the mall or the latest technology. Those are things that we use to try to find fulfillment. True fulfillment comes from within and one of the easiest ways to connect with our fullness – our essence - is through nature. Open your heart to possibility and join me on this great adventure into the world of trees.

Part II

Chapter One

~ Return to Nature ~

To be poor and be without trees is to be the most starved human being in the world. To be poor and have trees, is to be completely rich in ways that money can never buy.

~ Clarissa Pinkola Estes ~

This section consists mostly of direct messages that I have received from two different trees. They have named themselves Henrietta and George. I offer bits of information here and there but mostly let the trees do the talking. The italic print is my thoughts or questions and the remainder is from the trees. The messages are numbered for reference as opposed to creating a title for each tree message. Welcome to the 'juice' of this book – the world of conversing with trees.

1:1

Henrietta is beginning to feel like a friend. She shares so much with me not only with the messages that come through but also with the very tender, loving feeling that I receive from her. So when I approached this day I greeted her like I would any friend. I asked, ***"How are you Henrietta?"***

Asking a tree, 'How are you?' is a silly question. We have only one way of being and that is being. We do not have good days and bad days. We are. We exist. That is it. We witness that which is unfolding around us. We are aware of the noise of the saw and see that home repairs are happening close by. We notice a person walk by and observe their thoughts and emotions as they pass. We soak up the sunlight and feel the synthesis within our cells. This is our existence. Because we do not move, we cannot run away from what is as humans do. If someone approaches us with saw in hand we realize that we are about to serve the earth in a different way - perhaps as fire wood to warm the hearts of those who gather round the stove. They are warmed by our embers with no thanks for what we have offered. It is not that we need the thanks, for we are happy to serve in whatever way Creation brings to us. But mankind would do well to have appreciation - for its own evolution - its own connection to the All That Is. It is the loss of this connection that is a great part of the demise of humanity.

For you see, we are part of the Creator itself, as are you. We are part of the natural world that holds the core essence of the creative force of God, or All That Is. By connecting with us you are connecting with the origins of your soul. And so, as humans consume that which is derived from the natural world, it would serve them well to consider their good fortune in having this natural product to consume. Humanity, in its evolution away from the Light, has allowed itself to become very disconnected from the essence of nature. In its place is a yearning but no true understanding of what one is yearning for. The quest for connection has led to addictions. The empty soul seeks pleasure through lust, alcohol, drugs, TV. The list goes on. And it goes on because soul satisfaction does not come from these things. The deep yearning is for your true nature - your nature as humans connected to the Divine. There is more divinity in a tree than in most humans you see walking about - searching with empty eyes.

We are here to serve you. It is our greatest pleasure to support you in whatever way we can. Thankfully for us, the trees, we have our connection to Mother Earth. She sustains us as we do her. She appreciates what we offer to her carefully planned ecosystems. She is the great Mother - always looking to improve and grow spiritually so that she can lead her 'children' to ever greater heights. And so as we reach into the heavens, we are also deeply anchored into the earth. Our roots spread to embrace our Mother Earth and our branches reach up to give praise to our Father Sun. We are balance on this earth. Those who are in the cities are lost to this way of being. Therefore, it is those who live among us (the trees) who will be the first to see the way out of darkness. It is those who appreciate the beauty around them who also reflect that beauty from their hearts. They are the ones who will lead all of humanity out of the darkness.

And so as you sit at my base, remember these words. Life is precious. It can pass in a fleeting moment. Is it worth the headache and heartache that is your current way of being? Those who have stepped out of the rat race know the difference. Those who have stepped away from materialism are finding their way back to their hearts. It is not a big mystery. It is surrender. Surrender your life to simplicity. Stop running. Anchor yourself into the earth. Then your heart will be filled with joy. As you honor the earth and her creations you will be honoring yourself. In honoring yourself in this way you will feel the wholeness of life begin to bubble up in your essence. The deep yearning and emptiness will be replaced by fulfillment and wonder. Sadness will fall away to joy as you remember your true essence. This awaits you but you must make the choice. You can let the idea of having to sacrifice your current life keep you from this choice or you can realize that the only life worth living awaits you and moving toward it is not sacrifice but wisdom.

We are deeply delighted with the opportunity to share this knowledge with you today.

1:2

HENRIETTA

I would like to say what a blessing it is to have people listening to the trees. And because you are listening, I would like to tell you about the natural world. It is so much more than you give it credit for, so to speak. As humans you have diminished all life as insignificant compared to yours and yet we say to you that there is an intelligence that is nature that you do not understand. And so we could ask what has the most intelligence, animals, plants, or humans? We could say that it would be a toss-up. And the reason is that humans have become so cerebral that they have lost their true intelligence. Creating stressful lives and running in circles and having no time for one's self is not what we would call intelligent. It is in being like a tree, staying still and noticing what is around you, that you would come to find that you have much more contentment in your life. So, this thing that you call intelligence has actually led you away from your wisdom. We are happy to say that this will change now that you are shifting as a species. The energies of the planet on which you live have changed. Gaia is now resonating at a new level or tone than in the past.

For humans, and all life, this means that you are shifting as well. With this shift you are seeing people with more compassion for animals and nature. You are finding your way back to your true nature. You will then begin to love yourselves more and therefore love everything outside of yourself more as well. It is hard to say which comes first, compassion for the self or compassion for others, including the plant and animal kingdom. It is all connected. Trees and plants have always had compassion. We have been here, your sentinels of love, waiting to offer what we have to you. For those who are sensitive, you can feel our love when you hug a tree. And you can feel our love when you care for the land and appreciate the natural world around you. So, we are delighted that you are listening. Now you will know what you have been missing.

In the time when people lived off the land there was great struggle. Crops often failed and storms blew off roof tops. And yet, there was a much greater sense of satisfaction with life. People worked hard, working the land, growing crops and preparing for winter. Even though it was hard work, it was rewarding work. At the end of the day they could step back and look at something tangible that they had accomplished. They could see the garden growing and the preserves filling the cupboard. All these things contributed to the fullness of their day. And so, at day's end when they were tired, they knew they had accomplished something useful. And they felt the great satisfaction of working on the land, in harmony with nature.

Today you do not have those tangible rewards for your work. What do most of you see as a reward for a hard day's work? It is a silly piece of paper called money. And what does that piece of paper represent? For many it represents pain and hardship and lack. That is what you use as the symbol of your day's work. Can you see how this would leave you feeling empty? There is not the same sense of accomplishment for many, many people on this planet. We understand that some of you are living by doing what you love to do, but for most that is not the case. So, at the end of the day, there is no sense of satisfaction from your work. And then, most of you live in cities. There is no connection with the land. Many people go day after day without ever walking on soil. You walk on concrete everywhere, never touching the living grass or noticing the trees or seeing the flowers. It is that disconnect from nature that has so many feeling empty and desperate.

We are here inviting you to come back to your senses. Use your senses, not just your mind. Nature is very playful if you connect. You can feel the breeze as you walk from the bus to your work place. You can imagine that it is dancing with you, like a romantic lover. You can notice where a little weed is growing through a crack in the sidewalk and have proof of the tenacity of nature. You can feel the sun warming your back and know that it is providing life to you and appreciate that it is there. You can expand your world in this way and get out of the little box that is the mind. There is magic everywhere. Look for it and you will find it. Find it and your life will change. Slowly, day by day, you will change. You will feel more fullness from life. Take your children to the park, not the mall. Do not fill your idle time with more stuff. See if you can find the biggest tree in your community. What a fun activity for children. How many trees can you name? All the trees that are in your neighbourhood (hoping there are some) are waiting to be noticed by you so that they can offer their love to you. It seems like a fickle thought to many and yet, to those who know and who feel the love that is being in nature, it is not fickle, it is profound. You cannot see what you will not look at. You cannot feel love if you will not open your heart. And so it is with the trees, you cannot feel our love if you do not believe it is possible. For those who know it is possible, they are richer for it.

They are fulfilled in a way that material goods will never equal.

Your life doesn't need more stuff, it needs more love. No matter who you are you can find love in nature. Nature does not say you are not good looking enough or tall enough or thin enough or that you do not have the right job to be hugging a tree. Those are not the qualities that we see. We see your light. We see your love light. If it is dim we do our best to illuminate it for you. If it is bright, we dance with you. All of life is from the same source, and that source is love. If you are feeling lonely or frightened or sad, come visit us. Put yourself in nature and cry and let it out and know that we are hugging you with our love. We have no judgement for your fears – only compassion. Come visit. You are always welcome. And we will always love you, no matter what you do. That is what we are. Life just is. You would be surprised at how fulfilling that is. It comes from the very core of creation which is love. How does it get any better than that? Stop searching in your malls for love. Come outside to play. That's where the fun is.

I would like to share an experience that speaks to Henrietta's comment about the richness of connecting with trees. Recently I went to Toronto to offer a workshop and some dear souls whom I only know briefly opened up their home to me. Travelling alone has been a challenge for me in the past and I was determined that this time I would have support. Their generosity was that support. However, in order to give them some space I would go for a walk each day. I was in a beautiful part of the city and the streets were lined with trees and flowers in bloom. As I walked I would appreciate the trees and say hello to them and felt deep gratitude for the beauty that was unexpected in the city. Twice on my walk I found myself in tears even though I had no idea what they were about. The second time I just asked in my head, what is going on? Why am I so emotional? I heard the answer come back to me and then it made sense. I was told by the trees or by my higher self that I was sending so much love to the trees and plants that they were sending that love back to me. That form of love again, is so pure and powerful that I was walking down the street happy and in tears!

1:3

It's an overcast day – a little cool. I am not fond of the cold and so it makes me realize that I will not likely come to the trail as often once the weather turns. I will still connect from home and go to the trail for walks without doing my writing there.

I have noticed that I come here now with so much intention to write that I don't stay as present in the moment of just being here. So today I spend more time connecting with Henrietta before I begin to write and feel the exchange of love. This time I am consciously giving back ...

... and Henrietta begins: Giving and receiving. That is one circle of life. It is the way of it. You are given life – you receive life and then, at one point, your physical body gives back to the earth from which it was created. A tree receives life as the seedling is coaxed out of its shell by warm sunlight and moist soil. The tree grows, receiving light, giving life to the creatures that nest upon it or the bugs that crawl upon the bark. This giving and receiving repeats itself, over and over. And then, even as the tree loses its connection to the earth and falls to the ground, it continues to give. Fungi begin to sprout out of the bark and nutrients wash out of the decomposing wood into the soil slowly, ever so slowly, returning to the earth all that it was. Nothing is wasted. Nothing is worthless.

The same is true for the human body. Even when you burn the body after death, the ashes will return to the earth one day. And all the energy that was held together by vibrating atoms is returned to the energy field so that it may be used once again. So sacred is this cycle in the natural world that very few understand the beauty of it. In your human perspective you give value to the young and youthful and yet you choose the oldest tree in the forest to gain the wisdom that is tree. The cycle of life is misconstrued in this regard for humans. There are some cultures on this planet that have not lost the wisdom of this – what you would call the native or aboriginal cultures. But, for the so called civilized nations, this great truth of the wisdom of age is lost on you.

This wisdom is part of this cycle. As a tree ages, or an animal ages or a human who has found grace in the heart ages, they realize the beauty of the cycle and they find peace with it. They look at the young not with envy, but with patience. They remember what it was like to approach the world with so much enthusiasm – with abandon and passion. Then, in the cycle of life, that passion softens. It becomes wise and gentle. In that wisdom comes so much appreciation for what is that one could not imagine wanting anything else. The wise soul is one that accepts what is – being aged, perhaps loss of mobility that comes with that. They do not see it as a loss, they see it as an invitation to slow down. And by this grace the cycle unfolds easily and joyfully. Without resistance, life is able to flow with ease. So many humans resist the flow. They push themselves to be what they are not. They yearn to be thin when they are fat. They yearn for curly hair when it is straight. They yearn to live in Australia when they live in the United States. We are not saying that your life should not change or you should not maintain a state of wellness. It is what drives your desire for wellness. Are you in a state of wellness because you feel so alive with joy that you love to be active? Wonderful. That is living in fullness. But, if you are exercising because you are worried about getting older, afraid the body will stop moving or afraid you will become less attractive if you stop working out, then you are not living from fullness. You are pushing from a place of emptiness.

What is the greatest desire of all humans? It is to have joy. However, there is no joy in trying always to look like someone else or be younger or thinner. The joy comes from accepting what is. Accept the cycle of life dear humans. Walk through life like an ever changing forest path. Every step of the journey offers a new discovery. Why wish it would be different than what it is? That is not natural. It will not happen so you may as well accept the change that comes with the cycle of life. The more change you are witness to the more you have to share. That is why I am the speaker of this forest. That is why I am the one chosen to share the knowing. I have earned it. I have endured hardship to tell the tale and I have had the opportunity to provide comfort to those who stopped at my side. I have held a place of prominence on this path and so I give back. I give for it is as much a part of existence as being. I give by being. That is the deepest truth for all creation. We are one harmonious system designed to give and receive – give and receive. We would not exist without that flow. It is the breath of life. My breath is your breath. That is the giving and receiving.

So this is our conversation about cycling through life. Find your way back dear humans. Find your way back into your heart – your true nature. The whole world awaits you there.

1:4

Meet GEORGE …

One day as I was walking on a new trail I noticed a beautiful Norway Spruce. I was standing admiring it when I again felt an invitation to engage. The tree immediately presented as masculine and told me 'his' name – George – en francais s'il vous plait! He has a softer energy than Henrietta even though he chose a masculine nature. He is very loving as well. Here is one of my questions to 'him'.

"Henrietta has talked about humans finding their way back to their true nature through nature. Is there more that you can say about this?"

A delightful question indeed for humans have stepped far from their source being the earth and the sun. You have even been taught to be afraid of the sun. The sun is the source of all life. Without the rays of the sun falling upon this earth you would not survive. You know this and yet you have lost your connection to it. The same goes with the earth. You know that she provides everything you need to survive and yet, the way it is manipulated and bastardized, it is a wonder that you can survive at all. Many are finding their way back. It is becoming so obvious now that you are beginning to understand how far removed you are from the source of all life. This is a good thing. It is interesting that those who have done what they can to lead you away from nature and the natural way of existing, are the ones who have revealed their level of disconnect through the blatant and obvious manipulation of nature. So, they have created their own demise you could say. Now more and more people are standing up and making demands around food and the way that nature is 'managed'. This is leading you back to your true nature. It is happening because your withdrawal from nature is becoming more obvious. As people make choices for food that is organic and non-GMO, you are also bringing yourselves back to the natural world and developing an appreciation for mother earth and the sun in a way that you have not had for eons of time.

We know that there are many on the earth who would love a new level of existence – one where you are living more fully on the land, growing your own food, gathering your own eggs, etc. This is an existence that calls out to the hearts of many. In this way you will find your back. Like all cycles, it comes around full circle. You live fully off the land, you stray from the land, you come back to the land. Each part of the cycle is driven by a desire for something new. This is appropriate in the evolution of life. And each time you come back to zero point you start again at a new level on the spiral. So, although you appear to be moving in a circular fashion, it is truly a spiral. Yes, you move back to the same point where you started but at a higher level of existing at that point. This is where humanity is at this time in your evolution. You are coming back to zero point, ready to begin anew at a higher level than when you started this cycle. So, even though you may be moving gradually more back to the land, it will not be in the same manner that you lived in past times. It will be more 'advanced' you could say this time. You will not give up your technology, but you will put it to better use. You will use it to support your journey back to a healthy planet.

New technology will be coming very soon that will see you living in a way that can honor the earth and still have your needs met. No longer will you rape and pillage the earth for your survival. There is technology that can support all the population of the earth without causing her any harm whatsoever. Do not let the leaders of your countries tell you that this is not possible. It is and it already exists. Soon, with the uprisal and the demands of the people, more and more will be revealed. It will soon be safe to bring these inventions forward. It will be such a beautiful turn of events because you will be able to enjoy all the benefits of your technology and also be restoring the earth back to her pristine beauty. As you do, you will realize that your own beauty is sourced from the earth. You, as a human race, will begin to appreciate more of what is instead of thinking everything must be something else. An example of this is that you will begin to appreciate aging instead of thinking everyone must look youthful. This will come from appreciating the fullness of life. As you appreciate the fullness of life, you do not have the desire for anything to be different than it is. Each person will be respected and nurtured to be just who they are, with all their quirks and personality traits being appreciated for what they are. From this you will find much less violence on the earth. Violence comes from pain and fear acting out in the physical. When the young are raised from a place of acceptance for who they are and nurtured with kindness and gentleness, then they do not have to act out anything but love when they mature and make their way in the world. All this lies before you and as you find your way back to nature and your true nature. Your true nature is to be loving and kind. Right now this is taught out of you as you are raised in a society that compares the child to what they believe is the norm. If the child does not fit in somehow, then the child is taught to be different than its true nature in order to be accepted. This creates great pain and hardship and it is what you see around the world.

So I am delighted to speak of this and to share with you what lies ahead for you in the times that you are moving into. It is very exciting for you and for all of nature. We were on the brink of extinction. Most of you do not know that but it is true. The system almost crashed before it was rescued. And who rescued it? It was the humans who almost destroyed it. There would be no other way. That is the way of it. So, it is very beautiful to see that you have saved yourselves by saving the earth. Now is the time of restoration. Just as it was a long cycle that led you to the brink of destruction, so will it be a long cycle to restoration. And yet, it will immediately feel like a more gracious world because you have hit bottom and you are on your way back up. Everything feels better than it did on the bottom. So, dear humans, rejoice and follow your heart promptings that lead closer to the land – to the earth. It is like a teenager rebelling and then realizing how much s/he appreciates her/his parents. S/he comes back. So too you are coming back to your 'parents' in this level of creation – the earth and the sun. I hope you have enjoyed this transmission and look forward to connecting with you once again.

I went back the very next day to connect with George to expand my connection with the trees. This time I just asked what he would like to share.

1:5

GEORGE

I would like to tell you about the energies that a tree emits and how we connect to humans. When you walk by a tree, it knows that you are there and it sends out a field of Light or energy to you as you pass by. It is our role to be supportive to all of nature and so we do this to support you in your lives. We pull our energy from the All That Is the same way that you do. So, we can offer that energy to you. People who are particularly loving will receive a different energy than someone who has intent to harm. The point is that we respond to our environment and to the people in our environment. If you would like to receive supportive energies through the day, send your loving kindness and thoughts to the trees around you and they will send the same to you. Every time you see them or think of them, they will send loving energies to you. That is why people can live in seclusion in the woods for example, and feel so loved, without the need for human contact. As you know, humans can be very hurtful but you will not feel hurtful energies from a tree. By loving the trees in your surroundings, your surroundings will feel more loving to you. Your surroundings will feel more like your own little sanctuary as you relate to your trees.

The one who writes these words has fond memories as a teenager of her relationship with trees. They were her support. They are what got her through troubled times. She did not know the depth of it at the time, but she could feel their support and their love doing what they could to comfort her. Many of you, as you read this, will have similar memories. You dismiss them but in truth, it is the trees connecting with you and vice versa. So, we are sentinels of loving support for you. We keep you warm in the winter. We provide materials for your homes. Our energy stays within the lumber that built your home and so it becomes a part of your environment. So, you can relate to us in that way as well.

Fortunately we are all over the planet, each climate bringing forth different species. Oh the diversity of this beautiful earth is genius. Please appreciate it. There is so much wisdom in the evolution of the natural world. And there is so much of your soul residing there. The more you connect with it the more you connect with yourself. The more you truly connect with the natural world, the more you realize all that you are. All the emptiness will be lifted from you as you connect more with the earth. Even those of you who do not think that you have a strong connection to the earth, if you would allow yourself to spend more time in nature, you will find that you are more relaxed and just a little more content with the world. It is like therapy, being in nature - free, affordable, convenient therapy. Why not give it a try?

Could it be that reducing chronic illnesses related to stress is as simple as spending time in nature? I believe so! Just take my experience of feeling the love from trees and how it touches my heart. That love heals! This is available to everyone when we are willing to believe that it is possible.

1:6

GEORGE

You live in a magnificent world along with all that is on this earth. You humans often feel a bit lost trying to make life what you would like it to be and so I would like to address this with you today. You see, as trees we have no choices to make. We stand and grow and reach for the water with our roots and reach for the sunlight with our branches. We welcome birds and insects onto our branches and we watch the world go by, so to speak. We do not run or play. We just grow. And yet, if you touch the branches or the trunk of a small tree you will still feel the energy of youthfulness. You might wonder how that can be. A tree is a tree. And yet we say to you that trees not only have different 'personalities', they also have different ages and stages just like humans. You see, along with the years of standing and growing comes a certain maturity. After being in a place for a certain number of years, a tree comes to learn what its role is in that place. It comes to understand what its purpose is and what it can offer to the living creatures that surround it. So, a tree in your yard will come to watch over you and project a loving energy toward you and perhaps a protective energy. A tree in a park may feel that its role is more to be showy so that people will admire the park and feel that it is worth having in their community. Trees take on their roles relative to the area in which they are located.

Have you ever known a stand of trees to die all within a matter of years? This is not a common occurrence for trees yet it does happen. The author of these words visited the home where she grew up as a teen and all the stately maples that had surrounded the front yard had died. She knew immediately that the trees did not receive the same appreciation and nurturing that her family had given them and they died, and she was right. As trees adjust to their environment, if that environment dramatically changes, the trees can lose their sense of purpose and die. This is just another reason to love the trees in your area. Let them know that you see them and appreciate them. They will feel more important in their earth mission when you do.

We would like to speak of trees in a jungle. Trees in a jungle live very different lives than trees anywhere else in the world. Everything grows fast in the jungle, and so do trees. This changes the purpose and intention of those trees. Their purpose is more related to that of medicine. If man was still living with intention and healing from the trees and not allopathic medicine, you would understand that, when something has a medicinal purpose, it needs to grow fast in order to provide the medicine that is needed. That is why so many cures are discovered in the jungle compared with the rest of the world. When you fully understand this you will not be so willing to cut down so much of the jungle. The soil that is destroyed with the fires that burn down the trees is forever transformed. It will never be the same soil again and therefore will not grow the same kind of trees with the same properties ever again. It took eons of time, and certain conditions, to create that soil. Those conditions will not be repeated. You will have new soil and new medicines but this is also a great loss for you. The time will come when you will understand that and you will change your ways of forest management.

So, we hope that you will look at trees differently as this information comes to you. There is much more than you understand in the existence of a tree. Find out for yourselves. Stand with your back against a tree and see how you feel. If you are feeling not well, let a tree help you. It can support you both physically and emotionally. This brings us great joy when we can support you in that way. We are here to serve, and every way in which we can serve is a delight for us.

Thank you for this opportunity to speak of trees and to increase the understanding you have of our purpose and capability on this earth.

I once stood against a young elm (young being a relative term as it was a very tall tree) and felt so much energy running through me that I began to hyper-ventilate. I asked what was going on and the tree in turn asked me how many days it had been since I had ***not*** *had a coffee?!! It seems there was a good amount of clearing to do. I had taken up coffee again after about fifteen years of not drinking any.*

1:7

HENRIETTA

We the trees, have a deep love for humans. For you see, you have the capacity to carry much Love Light in your hearts, so that, when you pass us by, we can benefit from that Light. We can feel it and absorb it into our molecules and use it for sustenance. Just as your hearts have an energy field that sustains you, it can also offer benefit to those whom you encounter. Some humans do not 'see' the trees as they pass by and their Light is more closed down, with their focus in their minds. Others have wide open hearts, mothers in particular, and offer much love as they pass by. This is one way in which trees enjoy humans. It allows us to grow healthy and strong. And we would say that when you connect with us it also sustains you. We offer our love back to you when you are willing to receive. Those who take the time to stop and connect with us get a shot of love as they do so. This is how trees can comfort.

There are many around the world who have befriended a tree or many trees. There are people who are willing to risk their lives for the sake of a tree. They understand the Divine connection between humans and trees. Sadly, despite their efforts, they are often not able to help others truly understand that connection. Those who place money ahead of their values do not dare consider the connection because then they will not be able to use trees in the way that they do. It is hard to be aware of the consciousness of trees and spend the day cutting them down. One must block that from one's awareness in order to perform the duty of cutting down tree after tree. This is survival for the human, created out of fear of lack. They do not understand that they could use the trees for their benefit while standing and profit from them, or cut them in a sustainable manner. They do not understand that they are destroying the land that they wish to use by cutting all the trees. You have seen the results of this ignorance as entire acreages are washed away after the trees are cut, losing all the topsoil to erosion. Then, it is too late to correct the damage. We understand and yet we are happy to create more awareness of the relationship between man and nature.

We are happy to advise you that the more you connect to nature the more you are supported by it. If you were to put more faith into the knowing that nature provides everything you need, you would soon do everything you could do to protect every tree, every species. You do not need all the chemicals that have been created on your world. All they do is poison you. Nature provides and nourishes you. There is such an extreme difference between the two. Most of you are not aware of all the natural sources of medicinal drugs. The inspiration comes from nature and then it is corrupted and manipulated into something that is either non-beneficial or harmful. It appears to work for a while, but it leads to some other illness or problem within the body. Natural remedies are much the opposite. They come with the complete complement of attributes that lead to health in all aspects of the problem. They are holistic as opposed to segmenting your illness. What appears to be a liver problem could truly start in the stomach. By taking natural remedies, you will be benefitting both. How do you think aboriginal cultures survive in the jungle with no 'medicine'? They have the medicine of nature and they survive in wild environments in perfect health. They are at one with nature and therefore they live in harmony with all that is. It is a beautiful existence - simple, joyful and complete. They have not lost their spirit. It is part of their connection to the natural world. They live a spiritual existence because of their connection to the land. This makes them whole and harmonious. Their lives are not out of balance like many in the modern world.

Those in the modern world are discovering the land again. You are waking up to the simple pleasures in life. It is about giving yourselves permission to spend time doing nothing. That 'nothing' is really something when it is spending time in nature. Sitting by a stream on a summer's day is not a waste of time. It is the wisest use of time, for it stills the soul as it nourishes the heart. It connects you to your earthly mother. When you are in resonance with her, you are in good health – you are joyful and feel complete. This is what a summer's day by a stream can do for you. Get out into nature once again and find wholeness in your life. And take your children out of so many indoor activities and put them in nature. Take them to the woods and go exploring. Their growing minds will marvel in all that they see. They will touch the moss and feel its softness under their feet. They will smell the pine needles on the forest floor and inhale deeply. They will find twigs to use as swords of Light as their imaginations have time to expand into wonder as they become super heroes. This is much better for a child than another class that is indoors after being indoors in school all day. What better school is there than to expand the imagination? After all, you create with your imaginations. The more vivid the imagination is the more you can create. Take a child outdoors and give them the opportunity to step into the creative mind and out of the logic, structured state of being. Take them away from the smallness of their technological toys and expand them into the vastness of nature. Allow them to grow into their true nature through nature. You will be giving them a great gift. Do you think childhood memories come from the latest game for their technology? Gift your children with time in nature. It will bring your family together, if you choose to connect, for none of you will be distracted by other things. You will be there together, hopefully present in mind as well as body. Be conscious of doing this for yourselves and your children. Fully present in your mind as you step onto the grass and feel its coolness under your feet. Go ahead, be brave and walk in your bare feet. That is why you have skin, so you can touch things without harming the internal workings of the body. This is our invitation to you today. It is given with a deep yearning for humans to find their way back to the wholeness of who they are. You are of the natural world – of the earth. Remember who you are.

It amazes me that we are so disconnected from nature that we give terms like 'earthing' to describe what used to be simply called walking in your bare feet. It's like it has become some scientific method to discover. When I was a child people looked forward to going barefoot in the summer and loved the feeling of the grass under foot. One good thing about 'earthing' is that the research shows that one's health actually improves from connecting one's feet to the earth's energy. No doubt that is why we used to look forward to going bare foot in summer! We knew we felt better, we just didn't have a term for it.

1:8

HENRIETTA

Nature is the world made by the Creator of All That Is. Nature – in its pure state – does not come from the mind of man. It comes from that which many call God. We would refer to All That Is. It is because of this that we say that humans can find their way back to their true nature through nature. Much of your time is spent connecting with that which is man-made. This is especially true for those who live in cities. Your roads are man-made – your vehicles are man-made – your dwellings are man-made – your technology that is so much a part of your daily environment is man-made. Even your food is man-made to a great degree. So there is very little connection with what is natural. And what is natural has a divine essence because it came from Divine Mind you could say. This is why, when you connect with the natural world, it is a different connection. It takes you, if you will pause for a moment and truly BE with it, it takes you to a different place within your Being. It takes you out of your mind and into your heart. When you connect with something in nature, you feel good. It lifts your spirits. If you put your children in front of the TV for two hours they get cranky and start arguing with each other. This is not just sibling rivalry. This is spiritual deprivation. Their spirits need sunshine and fresh air. This is so lost in your current society.

Today it is important for parents to get their children outdoors as much as they can because many children spend much of their day indoors. When you look back to how children were raised 100 years ago you will see that children would come home only when they got hungry. Many would spend their whole day outdoors playing with friends in the natural environment. And we can assure you these children were never bored. They were as happy as could be. Compare this with the children of today and you will see what you have lost. It is your true nature as animals living on this earth to be more connected to the source of your life. The earth and the sun sustain you, like they do all life. The more you enter into the way of being with the earth the more life sustenance you will feel. We also believe that you will find more joy – the majority of you at least – by making conscious life choices to have more nature in your life. And where does joy come from? This is a question we invite you to consider.

There is love here waiting for you. We embrace you with our essence. Can you feel it? Ask your children if they can feel it in nature? But please do not ridicule them when they share what it means to them to connect to nature. Perhaps they know something you have forgotten. We, the forest, send love to you - Creator love. It is what we are and it oozes out of us like sap from the bark, ready for you to notice and here to serve your highest good, for we know why we are here.

1:9

I am sitting at a park today and connecting with Henrietta from here. I closed my eyes to connect and then opened them and there were two dragonflies close to my leg. Then one landed on my leg and here it sits, even as I write. It is a tiny red one. It leaves seemingly to catch a bug and then returns. It has done this several times now. Henrietta tells me, as I connect with her now, that the more I connect with the natural world the more it connects with me.

I 'chat' with Henrietta for a while, record her message and close my journal. Then, as if on cue, the dragonfly returns, resting beside me on the bench. At this point I tried to connect with the dragonfly. I was told that I had to connect with the over soul of dragonfly in a sense. I did, and a large blue dragonfly came into my awareness. I asked the meaning of the dragonflies coming to me. I was told that it was indeed to recognize my connection with nature. I asked about many people being attracted to dragonflies as a symbol of transformation. It told me that I am transformed – like one with the natural world. I had a sense of my cells morphing or blending in with my surroundings. I asked about the role of dragonfly and got the sense, similar to Henrietta and the trees, that it is to be. Very simple. It also said that humans would do well to notice – that so many are completely oblivious – lost in the busyness of the mind. It ended by saying that it is good for me to be sharing this – to help open the minds of humans to the possibility of existing in a deeper connection to nature.

HENRIETTA

Let us speak again of the natural world and of humanity's connection to that world – that 'system' that is planet earth. We wish to share with you the Divinity that is human connected to nature. For you see, it is through this connection that you find your way back home. It is through this connection that you find your true essence – for you are deeply connected to the earth. Your very physical being is created from the earth.

Long ago, in the times of LeMuria, you were At One with nature. Those were times of peace. For when you are connected to that nature – the nature of being human in full understanding of your earthly connection – then you have no desire to cause harm to anything or anyone. You are connected to the heart nature of all life. And we say that all life has a heart nature. To think that nature exists in this perfect balance (when unhindered) without wisdom is truly foolishness. The times that you are moving back to will embrace more of this understanding. As your unnatural systems fall away – the economy – the desire for manufactured goods – you will find yourselves being more content and more fulfilled - once you settle long enough to stop mourning the broken system that was and take a look at your new life with fresh eyes. Some of those who found themselves living in tents after the housing market crashed in the U.S. realized that they were not as miserable as they thought they would be. This is because they were forced to connect as community and support each other, and because they were forced into a simpler lifestyle that saw them closer to the land. You will be surprised at how quickly you can adapt to a change in lifestyle once you stop comparing your new life to your old life. Once you adopt a simpler lifestyle – which will be forced upon some – you will know within your heart that it is a more peaceful way of being.

What do you see for earth changes that may indeed force some into a simpler lifestyle?

There are many potential outcomes at this time. This itself is changing. In the past it would have been easier to make solid predictions. In these times, humanity is truly creating a different reality with each passing day.

However, we see that some changes will be inevitable. Where they occur on the earth again depends on the level of consciousness of the Beings who reside in different areas of the earth. You recently saw earth quakes in Iran. Does it surprise you that your Earthly Mother would feel the need for some clearing of the energies in Iran? It is like moving to a new home. The energies change. The same happens with natural events that move the earth.

What else would you like me to know Henrietta?

Do you remember when you stood before the sound healer in New York and burst into tears? She looked at you like you had lost it. But you knew what the tears were about. You knew that it was a recognition of that same gift within yourself – dormant but oh so ready to awaken. You can be that to others. They will see their Light within you and choose to shine as brightly. That is the gift of fully living in the Divine essence of who you are. Each and every one of you has this beautiful Light within. When gathered together in loving support you are the rainbow bridge that leads humanity into the new essence of who you truly are. Humanity is awakening to its God-self nature. (*Henrietta asked me to include this for the benefit of others who have had the same experience. To support us in stepping into the fullness of who we are and what we have to offer this world*).

That is our conversation for today.

As I walked away after saying good-bye I could feel Henrietta pouring her love out to me so strongly that I started to cry. It is a love that is unlike what we experience in this world. I also channel higher Beings of Light and the love from Henrietta felt similar to what I have felt from these Beings. It often moves me to tears as it touches deep within the heart, so pure and unconditional. Just love.

1:10

HENRIETTA

There was a time when people connected with trees all the time. You would call them the aboriginals. It was not always so with the pioneers of your country. It seems that they had worked the land, many times not in harmony with it, but out of fear of not having enough. On the other hand, the aboriginal communities honoured the land. You could say that they worshipped the land, and we would say that it was and is appropriate to do that. For you see, you are tied to the land in ways that you have lost awareness of. By worshipping the land, you also come to know the cycles of the land. You recognize the signs that tell you what the world is transitioning through. When that connection is lost, so too is your connection with your foundation. For who are you when the earth falters? Who are you when the grounds shake? It is then that you realize that you are indeed connected to the earth. When she takes dominion over you then you are soon shaken to a level of deep humility. It is only the love of the mother earth for all creatures that you have not endured deeper pain in this regard. And so by honoring the earth you are brought back to your source – to the source of your life. When you keep your connection to that then you are more connected with yourself. Your disconnect from nature is reflective of your disconnect from yourselves. Finding the fullness of nature is finding the fullness of self.

Those who entered this land from a more religious perspective were led by fear. They were led away from the true 'gods' of nature to worship a false God that would condemn you for your human nature and make rules that were unnatural. After a while you started believing so much that you managed yourselves away from nature. You took your heart out of the world and stepped into your mind, admiring and giving credence only to that which appeared to be intelligent. The truth is that the intelligence lies with those who still revere the land and who live according to her rhythms. They carry a much deeper intelligence than they have been credited with. By denying their teachings you have walked from the source of your life – the earth. And yet, she waits for you. She is a patient mother. She knows that you are on your way back, and none too early. Thankfully, many are giving up the false religions for the greater understanding of creation. Science that is not being denied is proving that all is connected and the mind is but a radar. As I have told you, humans have lost the understanding of how to pull their wisdom from the

All That Is, but that is returning. As you awaken you also are being led back to the truths of how existence really is created and where your true intelligence lies.

The more you connect with nature, the closer you are to your own deep inner knowing. When you can find deep appreciation for an acorn on the ground, then you arc finding the source of your presence on the earth. So, look for love in all the right places – in nature. When you find love there you will also find the love for yourself. **When you understand that everything in nature is perfect then how could you be anything less, for you are nature as well**. This is what is lost. There is so much hardship and pain from not loving the self. The solution lies in your connection to nature. Find your way back and find your way home.

These messages can seem so simple but if you rest on the words for a while you will come to understand that there is deep and profound wisdom here, like the sentence in bold above. We were created by a great and mystical intelligence that is far beyond our comprehension. To think of ourselves as anything less than perfect therefore is to dismiss the brilliance of creation itself. When we truly begin to understand this we will see the beauty in all things and all people.

1:11

HENRIETTA

It is a delight to have you at my base today, sharing your energies with me. There is a way of being in the natural world that leads to great peace when it is adopted by humans. That is the way of accepting what each day brings without knowing ahead of time what that may be. We understand that humans must do some planning – you get up and go to work every day – but your days would be more enjoyable if you allowed some space in your day for the magic to creep in. If you awaken each day expecting something unexpected you will find it. That something unexpected then begins to bring new life into your days and you begin to feel more alive. Life becomes very mundane when it is the same activity day after day. This magic that you will be looking for is similar to being more connected to nature. You may walk the same trail every day and yet it is ever-changing. One day you may see a red cardinal on the trail, another day a cluster of toadstools and another day more leaves have fallen. It is this change that keeps it interesting. The monotony of life can be overcome in this way by making space for the unexpected – what Rashana likes to call magic.

Awakening to the newness of every day leads to great joy. The life of wonder is one of possibility. If you awaken each day thinking that you know exactly how that day will unfold, you do not allow space in your mind to see the newness that is there. If you awaken with wonder you will at least open space for the possibility of new experiences. (*As I was writing this I had a vision of people travelling in a subway, empty faces, just enduring the journey and I realized it could be so different – perhaps smiling at a child or offering blessings in your mind to everyone around you*). Yes, the more you think of allowing something wonderful into that journey, the more possibility there will be for that. Life, in the human experience, has become very difficult for many. These simple practices can make a difference. Those who try them will find their lives changing.

And so this leads us back to your true nature once again. When man is living in the natural world there is wonder all around. One becomes attuned to one's environment and everything begins to synchronize. Life begins to flow in beauty and grace and appreciation blossoms. Life that is void of nature, with screens flashing and sirens glaring and people afraid to look each other in the eye – that becomes an empty life – hardly worth living. We would call it enduring, not living.

We invite you to seek magic in your day. What will the magic be in my day today? What new experience will I have today? When you ask the question you will be open to receiving.

I notice in this moment that the chickadees have come closer to where I am sitting in search of feed. They hang upside down and flutter among the branches. That is the magic for me. They are so cute and I feel blessed to be witness to their dance. It is this love of life that brings my soul alive ~ out of the mind and into the heart of creation!

Chapter Two

~ We Are Connected ~

What we are doing to the forests of the world is but a mirror reflection of what we are doing to ourselves and to one another.

~ Mahatma Gandhi ~

2:1

For the last couple of days I have been feeling .... a heaviness. Yesterday I would describe it as feeling guilty even though I couldn't find anything to be feeling guilty about. This morning I thought I might feel better if I went out for a walk. I headed down to the dyke where the wind was brisk and chilly, even though the temperature is above normal for this time of year. The view didn't give me the lift that I usually experience. On my way back I decided to head over to the trail where Henrietta resides. As soon as I entered the trail I felt better. Hearing the brook and being among the trees seemed to lift my spirits. When I reached Henrietta I gave her a hug and then leaned up against her trunk and felt the energy running through me. As I was connecting with her I wondered why I was feeling so out of sorts. Henrietta then told me that I was picking up on the fear that was floating around the planet with the pending December 21, 2012 date looming. That made perfect sense to me. There were so many predictions around the Mayan calendar ending on December 21st that there was a lot of fear connected to that date. So, I asked Henrietta to assist me in anchoring in the fear and sending it into mother earth to transform it into love. She suggested I ask all the trees of that forest to join in and so I did. I also called on the Sacred Fire to support us in changing the fear into love. After doing this Henrietta told me that the reason I felt better as soon as I walked into the woods is because the trees hold love. They are source energy, which is love.

That love was so present among the trees that it was almost like the mass consciousness of fear couldn't penetrate it. As I think about this, when the trees have told me that they can offer us protection, perhaps this is what they are referring to. They can create an impenetrable haven of love around our home on an energetic level. For people who are not so sensitive as to feel the energy shifts you can trust they are happening. It is like the canary in the mine. The more sensitive people are alerting others to the finer aspects of reality. With the awareness and desire to be in tune with the more subtle realities of our existence comes a growing level of awareness. When I first became a Reiki practitioner I couldn't feel the energies. I trusted that just because I couldn't feel it didn't mean that it wasn't there. Over time I started to awaken to it. Some of us, having shut down our feelings because of painful experiences in our past, can benefit from doing healing work that makes it safe to feel again. This helps us open up to feeling the subtle energies that are all around us.

I felt very different leaving the trail that day than when I entered. Just knowing that the energy I was feeling was not mine was helpful. I also realized for the first time what a powerful impact the trees can have on our emotional well-being. My sense of relief was immediate as soon as I entered the trail. Interestingly, I didn't feel it on the dyke where I am often deeply moved by the view. It was the trees that made the difference. We don't have to know why we feel better when we are in the woods or in nature, we just have to take ourselves there so we can experience it.

HENRIETTA

I would like to say to humanity this day that there is great hope now in the universe, for you to succeed in this great transition into the Light. Because you have passed the marker that was December 21, 2012, you have moved more fully into the understanding of what it is to be human. You will begin to see more and more care and concern for the environment and less tolerance for that which is harmful to the environment. This is because humans are awakening to their true connection to the earth and all of her systems. As you have more understanding of the hologram that is life, you will care more for the source of your life. You will also come to understand that the sun is not something to be feared but revered. Of course you know that you would not survive without it but there is much more to it. The sun is a source of wisdom and this will become more evident to you as well.

The world is changing. It is improving you could say. You are moving back to the awareness that all life is connected. Just like the roots of a tree reach out and connect with the tree beside it, your energy fingers – your auric fields – reach out to touch each other. Your auric field is 55 feet in diameter when it is healthy. This means that you are always connecting energetically with those around you. Even those living in apartments next to you that you may have never met in person, you are connected to. When you begin to understand this more you will change the way you live. It will begin with your connection to nature and a deep respect for all that is. This includes the creatures of the earth, the water, fellow humans, plants and all life. Once you begin to understand the deep connection that you have to all you will want to take better care of the all.

We, the trees, see this happening now. We see it in the circle of time. It has already expanded to this awareness and humans are already appreciating all life and loving all. It is mending the hearts that have been in pain for so long. As you find your way back to nature, you are softening. As you care for all life you are caring deeply for yourselves. This is the beauty of what is happening now. The more you love all life the more you love yourself, and vice versa. This is so beautiful. We can feel it so to speak. That is to say, we can understand the feelings that are unfolding in humans. It is like coming out of a cave that you have lived in all your life and walking into the sunlight for the first time. It is so joyous and warm and comforting. We see humans living simply, with great appreciation for each other and hearts full of nothing but love and the desire to share that love. It is like, in your progress, you are moving back to a more simple life. And every element of life is adored. You adore the water and the wind and the fire. Not like they are false gods but that you understand that they are part of your creation and that they have their own true nature.

Life is evolving now into a time of peace and grace. It is an evolution of love and we are so excited to know that humans will soon be honoring the earth the way they did eons ago. The aboriginal cultures have not lost this love, but most humans have. You are finding your way back now.

What can you tell me about water and how our appreciation and understanding of water will change?

Water is an element that stands alone in its energetic make-up and its characteristics. It is a fluid, solid, gas as you know. It is also an all-knowing state of existence. It can store memory much like a crystal. It can support you in your own growth if you but ask it to. Before you drink a glass of water ask it to be something for you. You can say to the water, “Thank you for clearing my infection.”, and the water will hold attributes that will clear your infection. You can say to the water, “Thank you for purifying my blood.”, and it will purify your blood. It has a wisdom that man has not yet fully accepted is possible. It is here to serve all life on the planet. It has been breathed by ancient Gods and modern man. It lives in the ocean and it lives in the air. It travels the earth and touches all life in the journey. Polluting your water without discrimination is a terrible crime. You would soon die if you were not to begin very soon to have respect for the water. Because you are mostly water, you are also polluted. This is reflected in your cancer and other illnesses and diseases in your modern time. When you clean up the water, you will also clean up your physical bodies and return to a greater level of health.

There is much that you will be discovering about water and how to use it to serve you. Purify your water and you purify yourself. Bless your water and you bless yourself. The demands to stop fluoridating the water are very good. The water is being destroyed and then called suitable for consumption. As humanity wakes up you are beginning to see all the manipulation that is destroying your health and that of the natural kingdom that supports you. We are delighted that this is changing. It is time. Do not trust others to tell you what is good for you. Listen to your own intuition and knowing.

This is such great wisdom to learn to trust our own inner knowing. We have been socialized to ignore our intuition. It has been labeled as flighty and ungrounded.

The truth is we are animal in nature and animals have an inner knowing and a level of awareness that goes beyond the physical senses. When we start to trust that again we are also trusting the unfolding of our life experience. We can let go of the need for control and allow life to flow. It opens up the potential for a whole new way of being. Life is constantly offering up new opportunities but if we are rigid in our thinking and not trusting the intuitive aspect of the self that nudges us toward those new opportunities then they are missed and life is just a constant flow of yesterdays.

2:2

GEORGE

It is a new year and humanity is changing. Would you like to speak of these changes to humanity and all life upon this planet?

Very well. I can speak of what is envisioned for the earth and humanity in these times. We see it as a shift where mankind is making its way into the new energies that are unfolding on this planet at this time. You have passed through the Precession of the Equinoxes and this is a grand marker in the evolution of the earth and all planetary systems when they pass through the center of their galaxy. Everything shifts with the passing of this event. The changes come slowly, but come they do. There have been times in the history of the earth when the change came swiftly, with the onset of an ice age of such dramatic climate change that all life was lost. As you well know, this was not to be the case for this passing of the cycle. This, in itself, is delightful. It is a new way, to allow life to remain while the earth goes through this portal you could say. It is very exciting for all life to have this experience.

What this means to mankind is that, being in the new resonance of the earth, things must and will change.

Because you have moved into a higher level of resonance on the earth (*the frequency of the earth is now at a higher resonance than the past several hundred years as science has discovered*) things must change. When you passed through the December 21st portal of 2012, you started this journey out of darkness and into a new way of being that is more connected to the Divine. So, as you move into these energies more fully, year after year, then you will find that everything is changing. This will include your monetary system, your communities, and your political leaders. Everything will change because what was no longer resonates with the new level of being. It is like a child growing out of its clothes every year. You know that they are changing as they grow and so you do not begrudge having to buy new clothes for your child. It is the same for humanity and its way of being on the earth at this time. You are growing and learning how to be in these new times. As you do so, you will be growing out of many of the outmoded models of existence that have been anchoring you into darkness. Now is the time to walk out of that.

For humanity it means the need to be flexible and accept the changes that you see all around you. It must happen. Resisting it will only make it more difficult. The more people can flow with what is, the easier their lives will be. We, the trees, would highly recommend walking among us to make this transition easier. For you see, we do not resist what is. We know what is unfolding on the earth and we accept all that is. Because of this, we remain in the constant state of love and so being with us will allow you to feel that love. You will feel the harmony of non-resistance that is the trees. You will feel the stillness. By being in nature, you will allow yourselves to walk in this harmony as well. You will come to appreciate us more than you have in the past. You will look at us differently, for you will see the qualities of yourselves there. You will see our branches reaching into the heavens and see that you also desire to be connected to the All That Is. You will see our leaves flourishing and growing as spring moves into summer and you will see that you too feel more celebratory as summer approaches. You will see our branches reaching out to touch one another and you will appreciate those around you. By being among us you will find your own self. It is the stillness of being in nature that will bring you back to your own center.

Life is challenging for some and purely joyful for others. It is what the personality looks for that will make this difference. Do not believe in luck. It is a false idea of destiny. It is your beliefs and expectations that create your life. Look to those who appear lucky and study how they live their lives. There is much to learn from them.

As a healer I see the truth of what George has offered. I see that those who have done their healing work and have found self love are creating beauty in their lives. Those who are struggling and focused on what they don't want are seeing more of what they don't want! We are manifesting very quickly in these times so it is indeed important to learn from those who have found their way into joy.

2:3

It is a glorious fall day! When I first approached Henrietta she asked me to sit in silent prayer for this forest. My mind expanded beyond here and she pulled me back. I was about to speak a blessing and she said 'silent prayer'. So I behaved and we sat in silence for a moment.

And so it is Rashana that again we find ourselves together. And glorious it is to be with you. For you see, as you befriend the forest, the forest befriends you. If ever you needed comfort you could come here and it would be given. And how does one befriend a forest? Not by rallying your government to protect the trees (although that is appropriate at times). Not by bringing all your friends to sit and party with the trees. You do it in stillness. You do it in the stillness of your heart as you walk among the trees and notice. Oh how bountiful your harvest you may say to the great oak. Keep reaching for the sunshine you could say to the little seedling. Your praise and encouragement would be received with the same level of joy that comes to a child who is praised by a loving parent. As you hear the wind, liken it to the blood pumping through your veins. Do you not breathe the oxygen that we emit in exchange for the carbon dioxide that you breathe out? Could there not be a clearer example of how we live in harmony? The air you breathe has been breathed by people around the world. It has filled the lungs of the farmer in Japan and provided the only sustenance for the starving child in Africa - one source - one life - many forms. That is the way of it Beloved Rashana. All can find their way back to this. It is available to all who will open their hearts to the joy of it.

This is a day of great magnitude on your Earth. (*When she said that I thought that there may be some planetary alignment that she would tell me about or something happening that I was not aware of. Instead it was a lesson in appreciation*). The sun is shining brightly unhindered by the clouds. The breeze blows through the leaves as they sway and flutter with appreciation. The shadows play upon your paper as the pen glides. This is the poetry of nature - ever changing, ever growing and ever evolving. So, you humans who read these words, bring yourself to us. Allow us to merge with you, even for a moment. Do not come to feel sorry for us. We are at peace. Come to feel that peace. Come to rest in the love we have to offer. It will open you heart so that you may find that peace within yourself.

2:4

GEORGE

I am delighted to have this opportunity to speak through you today to all those who will read these words. We, the trees, are delighted that we can speak to so many through Rashana. We carry wisdom that is seldom recognized. We understand the way of the natural world. We witness the way of the human, in your state of being disconnected from the natural world around you and we have less understanding of that. It makes us sad, you could say, that humans do not fully accept the opportunity to use trees for their benefit. For you see, not only do we give you oxygen to breathe, but we give you energy. There is a great energy exchange between humans and trees. We have the ability to turn the energy of the sun into green growth. Humans do not use the sun in this way, and so the energy we give off in that process, benefits you. This has not been studied before, for no one has thought to do so. We invite your scientists to study the energy that is transmitted off of trees and how it is of benefit to humans. There is an exchange in this way as well. We can support you, and we do, but you are not aware of our support. It is why people feel so good when they live among the trees.

Humans also need sunlight, so it is not good to allow the trees to keep you constantly in the shadows, but it is good to have trees around you. In your cities trees are planted to beautify your city and to make people feel better about where they live. We are an essential part of the human experience. The energy we give off is life-giving, just as oxygen is. We can support your life force with our life force. We stand tall and gather the life force energy of the earth and the sun. With our ability to do this, we have much to offer to you as well. Touch a tree and you can feel this energy run through you.

This is one way in which humans can benefit from being more connected to nature. You are, but you have forgotten. With this wisdom coming forward, you will develop more understanding about the symbiotic relationship that we have. You support us and we support you. Nature has many systems which function in this way. It is the way of harmony. It is the way of the natural world. Even as you see animals killing for their survival, as humans do, know that it is a harmonious relationship even though it ends with death for some. Nature knows that balance must be maintained for the highest benefit of all. However, in the natural systems, much of this balance is voluntary. Many species produce young in accordance with the availability of food. There is a natural respect for the environment and young are not brought into the world where there will not be enough to sustain them. Species other than humans respect the balance that is required for the sustenance of all. Humans, however, think only of their place in this hierarchy and do not consider the needs of those lower on the food chain. Humans do not even consider the need for balance. Much of what you do is out of balance. You find a nutritional substance that is beneficial and you isolate it from the source. You magnify its potency and use it that way instead of understanding that the food that originally contained the vitamin or whatever the nutritional substance is had many key components that allow the body to efficiently use the nutritional value of the substance. This is one example of how you are out of harmony with nature and now you are seeing your bodies very much out of balance, with many illnesses and emotional disturbances affecting humans at this time.

By finding your way back to the natural world, and learning about how things work in nature, you will rediscover the truth of who you are as humans in relation to the earth. There was a time when all lived in great harmony. It was a time when life was simple. There need not be technical advancements that lead you away from nature. You can use your technology to be in harmony with nature as well. It is the choices you make that lead you far from this balance. Come back to your source of life. It is like returning home after a long dispute. Find your way back to the natural world by being interested. Come stand by a tree, touch the trunk and see what you feel. If nothing, that is OK. Send your love to the tree and know that it will be felt and returned to you ten-fold. Nature has a lot to give but it must be respected. All resources can be depleted when thrown out of balance. Humans have proven that. Look to nature for evidence of harmony and then ask where you can recreate that in your own lives. This would be good for humanity at this time.

I would like to end by saying that we are waiting. We are excited to think that humans will find their way back to nature through the trees. We are waiting.

How beautiful to think that the trees are waiting for us, anticipating our connection like a patient and loving parent, waiting for a lost child to return.

2:5

HENRIETTA

The landscape has changed since my last visit over a week ago. The ferns have all died down and the leaves on the ground are turning brown. As I sit on Henrietta's roots and close my eyes I realize her energy is going right up through my root chakra!

Her message today is about the power of love. She says:

Love is the key to all creation. Creation is Love made to reflect love out into the world – to each other. Love all around. What a beautiful world that would be. Love cannot heal if people do not let it in. The power of love can conquer all but it takes a willing heart, one that has recognized that love brings life and is the true place of power. Evil has no power over love. If you only knew that you would laugh at the folly that you have lived, letting fear hold you back for so long. This is a reason to love the self. Step into your power of being love and stand strong in the Light of love like a warrior for Spirit. Strong are they who feel so much love from the Divine that they are invincible. They are invincible not because the physical body cannot be harmed but because the Spirit cannot be harmed. When you realize this you carry the strength of love and your life changes. Gone are the days of holding fearful thoughts. They are replaced with a knowing of the power that love brings.

When beings respond from love they feel more love for themselves. Love begets love, just as fear begets fear. The choice of where to reside in that lies within the one who is. Many become resentful and hold their love back because it was not given to them. They just keep it from themselves by doing so. When you hold love back from another, you are really holding it back from yourself. When you offer love to another, you are really offering love to yourself. This is a good way to create more love in your life. Offer more love out. Be loving to more people. You will, once you are willing to give up resentment, begin to see more love show up in your life when you do this.

Nature is love. Nature does not judge the sun for being too hot or the rain for falling too hard. It accepts all as perfect.

2:6

GEORGE

You presented yourself to me as a masculine version of tree. Can you tell me why?

Hello Rashana. Hello, hello, hello. I have been calling out to you for days, so when you think of me, know it is most likely because I am thinking of you and ready for some contact with you. It is my great delight to be called upon to express whatever it is you wish to know and so I will answer this question for you. I came to you as 'male' so that you would accept that aspect of reality and come to know that male energy can feel soft and gracious. For indeed, you remarked that you felt that from me in our first connection. It was my way of helping you and supporting you. For you see, when a human notices a tree and truly makes a connection, then the tree wants to give back. We are here on this earth to serve in many ways. We can channel energy from the All That Is and offer it to the humans who will stop and notice. And so it was my delight to offer that energy to you.

And now I hear in your mind that, when I say it is my delight, you question that sentiment because it is like an emotion. Please know that I am putting things into your way of understanding. Henrietta has her own personality which, ironically, is more rigid and 'masculine' than mine. Do you see what we are offering you here? You are in times when the world is ready to switch from a highly patriarchal system to a matriarchal one. This switching of the gender roles, you could say, is representative of that energy. So I come to you in softness and I am willing to offer you words of expression that would seem to have emotion. It is really a way of identifying with what I am offering as information to you.

When you say that trees are here to serve, in what ways are you able to do that?

Good question indeed. We can serve in ways that you would never imagine. For you see, we have a deep connection to the All That Is and we understand much more about the world of particles, the quantum world, than you do. We can gather up energy to support you energetically. We can nourish you with our bark. We can protect you from harm. If you are connected to the trees around you and in your area of living, you can receive intuitive messages from the trees that can keep you from harm or send ideas that inspire you. For instance, if there are trees outside your window, you can connect with those trees every day with your intention and those trees will stand as sentinels of protection for you. They could nudge you in your sleep if someone were lurking outside, they could send out an energy that would be repulsive to one who may intend you harm. These things seem impossible to most humans because you have lost this connection, but when Henrietta told you that she watches over you, this was the truth. We delight in caring for humans in this way. *(I just connected with Anastasia to confirm what I was receiving. If you have not heard of her, there are a series of books written about her and a web search will bring up the information you need. Her comment was that if the trees can connect with me they certainly can connect with the angels or my higher guidance if I have asked for the protection and am willing to receive it. As an aside, she connected with George and, as she did, I could feel his love for me as she was connecting with that energy. It almost brought me to tears.)*

What else would you like the readers to know?

Well, that is another question indeed. You are giving me permission to go wherever I would like to go with this. Hmmm… let me see. OK. Let us talk about love. Oh yes, love again. For indeed Rashana, have you not just today stated that your mission is to bring messages of love into this world? Indeed you have, so why would you be surprised that another message of love is coming to you? Can there be too much love in the world? I can't imagine why such a thing could be true. Love is all there is. Love is the reason for existence. Love is what keeps your molecules together. Without love you would just be a bunch of particles floating out in space. So, how could love ever be a topic that is spoken of too often? Indeed, it is not spoken of often enough, at least in the deeper understanding of what love truly is. For you see, love truly is the essence of all life. It is love that opens the petals of a flower. It is love that calls the humming bird to feed of its nectar. It is love that causes hunger in the wolf. It is love that heals the tears of a child. It is also love that harms the child and starves the wolf and kills the flower. You just have trouble seeing it that way.

There is love behind everything - it is just that you humans like it more when the love feels good. And yet, if you stay with your pain long enough with enough sincerity, you will find the love there, just as you did only a few days ago Rashana. You saw the gift of the pain that kept you out of your body for most of your life. You fully understood that the gift of your detachment allowed you to develop your deep ability to channel so clearly. And, when you had that understanding, you could see the love in the pain that had forced you to detach for so long. What an incredible gift that is. For when a human can see love behind the darkness, they have mastered the human existence. And that is where many of you are headed in these times. That is where the earth is headed. Mother Earth, in her great love for all the life forms upon her surface and below it, knows well of this. She has endured more than you truly are aware of in her service to all. On the brink of destruction, she still waits for you. She holds out for you in the hope that one more person will travel with her into the higher realms of existence. Oh, the magic in the understanding of which we speak. It is beautiful indeed. It thrills me to speak of it. For it is my hope then that it will spark curiosity in those who read these words so that they will explore what is written here. So thank you Rashana for the opportunity to speak of this.

Chapter Three

~ Tree Wisdom ~

There is always music amongst the trees in the Garden, but our hearts must be very quiet to hear it. *~ Minnie Aumonier ~*

3:1

Today Henrietta offers something very different from what she has given before. It is a seemingly simple story and yet, Henrietta has great wisdom. I invite you to consider what is underlying this story. What is the gift that she has shared with us this day?

Once upon a time there was a young lady who loved with all her heart. She was alive in the romance of her imagination. Everything in the world was romantic to her. She dreamed of her handsome prince. And you know, he came along. He showed up because she dreamed of him. She created him as her experience. She had a pure and loving heart and it called to her true love. She was radiant after finding him. Her face was so joyous that others were forced into a smile at the appearance of her. The love that flowed from her radiated out like sunshine. As she walked down the street she lifted the world. Each person who passed her by was touched by love. She was changing the world. Every word she spoke carried tones of kindness. Each breath she took was filled with gratitude. She lived in a world that many not dare dream of and that is why she was different. She dared to dream. She believed it was not only possible but that it would happen for her. She was the enigma.

She and her prince lived a long and happy life together. They had children and pets and gardens. They cared for each other and they cared for the land. They cared about their grandchildren and their neighbors. They did not buy into the fear that the media tried to send them. They did not buy into the lack that was apparent in their world. They focused on their love and their abundance of joy. They lived their entire lives this way. When they died so many came to pay their respects that they had to have two ceremonies. One ceremony was of the people who knew them dearly. It was those who had the privilege of seeing their lives intimately and knew how they lived. Those who knew them well did not mourn, they celebrated. For they knew that the dear couple was not gone, they had just moved to another experience. They knew that they could still connect in their hearts. Instead of feeling a loss, they celebrated the lives of this couple and all that they showed the world with their love.

The other group was mourning. For you see, the other group did not live close enough to the loving couple to fully understand the magic that they had. They only saw them passing on the street or they served them in one of the stores. They saw them out and about and knew of them but did not know them intimately. This group mourned. They mourned because they believed that the world had lost something. They did not see that the lovely couple was an aspect of who they are. They did not see the same qualities within themselves and therefore they thought that the world had lost something. The first group did not mourn. They knew the world had gained something and that the couple had also shown them something about themselves. The mourning group did not see this. They saw only loss. They did not have the experience of finding that love within and so they mourned.

That is my gift to you this day Rashana.

3:2

GEORGE

The art of being human is often a tricky thing. A tree has very few duties or responsibilities. It grows and supports other life and stands guard. A human however, has many things to learn and must take on many responsibilities and must continue to change all the time. You have children that you must care for and they grow and change continually. You attach to them as babies and must release them as young adults to find their own way. You are employed so that you can earn a living and take care of yourselves. You live busy, active lives with very little stillness. This is what brings much of the despair and hardship in your society. It is the lack of stillness.

When you think of nature, what do you usually think of? For most people it is stillness. Of course everyone knows that nature has two sides, like all things in a duality existence. Nature can be calm and still and it can be outrageous and destructive. That is the balance of existence. We would say that the realm of nature is more stillness than destructiveness. And yet, the human experience is more of a disruptive pattern of living than stillness. Most humans find very little time in their lives for stillness. And so, it is like their lives are similar to a continuous storm. Imagine day after day walking outside into a storm. For months on end, every day you walk outside and it is stormy. In the winter it is snowing and the wind is blowing. In the summer it is rainy and the wind continues to blow. You are always cold and always feel that you must harden yourself to stand against the winds. This is what it is like to be a human in these times. You have created lives that are like living a storm every day. It is the storm of hurriedness and busyness and demands of your careers and travel to and from work. You get home and then the children's activities begin and you gobble down some food and run out the door once again into the storm. This has created much weariness within the human body and psyche.

When was the last time you sat on your doorstep and talked to a neighbor? What, you say? Sit on my doorstep? Talk to a neighbor?? For many of you this would be unheard of. And yet, it would bring you great comfort. It would bring you a sense of belonging – a sense of community. Oh, but your closed hearts will not allow such a thing. This is brought forward to give you an idea of what we are talking about here. The little things that bring the heart pleasure, the slowing down of living, are far from the current reality for so many people on your planet. This is not to say that such people and communities do not exist, because they do. But, there are very few of them in your busy cities. Your city folk have lost touch with the stillness of life. The very thought is repulsive. Many are lost in the hustle bustle because it means that they do not have to look inside. They do not have to stop and wonder who they are. That would be terrifying in itself, and so they continue to run in circles, like a lab rat in a maze, running from the very essence of themselves.

There is much beauty in simplicity. We see that you are slowly finding your way back to that. And when you do, the trees will be here waiting here for you. We will be here noticing. And we will say welcome back. Welcome back to you. For you see dear humans, you are running from yourselves. And the only place where you will find true joy is within yourself. Therefore, you are running away from joy. We are here to help you and guide you. The natural world, in all its intelligence, is here waiting. Walk up to a tree some day and, in your mind, say hello. See how you feel. Do you feel that tree acknowledging you with its loving essence? All of creation is love. Because we do not have the experience of being out of the simplicity of merely being, we have love to share. That is what we are. **That is what all of creation is, unless you create otherwise, and even that is love.** So, when you acknowledge a tree and offer your love to a tree, you will get it back. If you can slow down long enough to still your heart you will feel it. Try it. It is not for the trees that we ask this. The trees do not need your support. We are full within ourselves. And we have love to share. It is for your experience that this is suggested. It is so that you can experience the fullness of the very world that you live in.

I would like to comment on the bolded sentence above. I have come to realize in my own healing journey that what appears as hardship and struggle is truthfully an opportunity to see what is wanting to be released from our belief system so that we can clear and let go of what is holding us back from the great joy and potential of life. I have done so much healing that I welcome the challenges as a gift, revealing to me the next level of the past that wants to be healed so that I may rise ever higher into the place of loving the self. So when George speaks to us 'creating otherwise' and that also being love, this is what is being referred to. All our experiences are coming from love, it is just that we don't always recognize hardship as such. In truth it is our Higher Self bringing opportunity for growth and expansion.

3:3

GEORGE

If you could say anything you wanted to a human what would it be?

That is interesting Rashana. There is much I would like to say. The first would be to notice. Notice what is around you. Get outside of your head and see the world that surrounds you. Many of you are so busy in your thoughts all the time you may as well never leave home. You are looking inside, listening to your busy thoughts that are really just going in circles, spinning around and around in your heads and never seeing outside. Use your eyes to look. Look into the distance, what do you see? Look outside of you but close up, what do you see? Truly look around you. This would be the first thing that I would say. Your world will begin to feel bigger when you do that because you will actually be expanding your awareness by looking outside of yourselves. It will surprise many of you how different you will feel just by doing this one activity. Then, as you begin to truly see outside of you, look at the finer aspects of what you see outside of you. At first you see a flower garden as you walk by it every day. Then, look onto the soil of that garden. What do you see there?

Are there bugs, fallen petals, spider webs? What microcosm is within the macrocosm that is garden?

As you begin to do this in nature, you may find it expanding into other areas of your life. How many of you truly know the nature of those around you? We could say that some of you do not even know your own children. You are so busy making supper, putting them to bed, getting them ready for school, and running out the door only to pick them up later for their extra-curricular activities that you have no time to stop and 'see' who they truly are. So, this can apply to many areas of your life. Stop and take the time to get outside of your head and into your life. That would be the first thing that I would say.

Another thing that I would say to people is to laugh more and enjoy life more. Stop taking yourselves so seriously. Life is meant to be playful and joyful, especially for humans. You have the nature to be light and carefree yet your lives of being so busy and so away from nature, make you very serious. This will change soon. You will come to realize that it is the love of family and community and life itself that is precious. You are so far removed from that now that your values are misplaced. That is going to change. The world of shopping and looking young is a narrow perspective. As this changes you will come to have a greater appreciation for the older members of your society and a deeper appreciation of the simpler things in life, like sharing with one another. As the world changes and things become simpler, you will find that the joy factor rises. There are people in the world who live in dire poverty and are much more joyful than most westerners. It is because they still have the values of connecting with one another and finding their joy there.

So, ask a tree what they would tell you and this is what you get. We see the way people are in this world. We would be happy to be noticed and to share our love with you. First you must see us. You will not see us if you never lift your heads to look around. There is so much to see outside of yourselves. After all, we are your creation. Why not look outside and see what it is that you have thought up. Mother Earth will appreciate your noticing as well. She sustains us all. Every time one of you notice, she rejoices, for she feels that love that you have for her. It sustains her just as she sustains us. Send her your love by loving a tree or a flower or the sky. It really is you loving yourself, for we are all connected. This is my message to you this day. Go visit a tree. Connect with it in your mind. Appreciate it and see how you feel. We are waiting. You can heal the planet very quickly with your love. Start now.

3:4

HENRIETTA

Today I would like to talk about earth cycles. Here you are in the mid of autumn and still enjoying 17 degree centigrade weather. You are enjoying this delightful warm period during this typically cold time of year. This is a cycle changing, much like the entire earth is changing. This is part of global warming and also part of a larger cycle of change. As your poles move, so does the climate. Where it once was cold becomes warm and vice versa. This is part of a very long cycle that happens on this planet and we are at the end of that cycle once again. At other times this cycle was cataclysmic but this time it will not be so. This time the cycle will be more gentle. This is because you are going through an evolutionary upswing.

The cycle where you are now sitting is changing itself. It is rising up in the realms of resonance so that it is able to occur with less loss of life on the planet than has happened in the past. So, there are many cycles. The cycles of the seasons on the earth and the cycles of longer evolutionary swings. With this grand cycle that is ending now, humans are finding that nothing is the same as it was. Time is changing, the weather is changing, some species are leaving and other species that have not been seen for hundreds of years are appearing. Everything is in the cycle of change right now.

I say to you that the cycle of love is before you. As you watch the seasons change and the leaves come and go, know too that the seasons of love change. First you are a newborn babe who receives love from its parents and revels in that. Then you grow into a child and your world expands and you develop love for more relatives and siblings. That love then grows out to the larger community as you go to school and develop friends. Then you become aware of your sexuality and love changes again. It is an ever-changing cycle. Even as adults, love changes. There is the infatuated love that is truly lust. There is the romantic love of your partner. Initially they can do no wrong and then it changes and your loved one begins to reflect all that you are to you - the shadow side as well as the more endearing qualities. That love then matures into the quality of love that comes from years spent caring for another. All this could be called the seasons of love.

To many, love seems stagnant but that is only a reflection of yourself. If your love of self stagnates then you will see it in your life. The cycle would like it to change but some resist the change and then they miss the season. In nature, there is no stopping the seasons of change. There is no saying mother earth, we would like summer to stay this year. It is an intelligent system that runs harmoniously when the change is allowed. And as we have told you, most of nature would never consider trying to change that beautiful cycle. Only humans, with their intelligence, believe that they can change the system. You are the only species that would try to manipulate all the other systems of the earth to meet your own needs.

Right now you are at the cycle that is 26,000 years long. It is a grand cycle of time that always comes with change. It cannot be any different. It is such a huge energy shift on the planet that it must come with great change. If you are at peace with what is then you have every reason to be very excited about this change. If you are one who resides in fear then you will find much to feed your fear. The fear comes from lack of understanding. Each of you has the ability to connect with 'the field' and find the answers to what is truly happening on the earth at this time. If you were to do so you would know that this cycle is not going to be like the others. You have graduated, so to speak. You have earned the right to remain while the earth goes through her changes. The storms you see and the earth shaking, it is all part of this shift. If it were going to be cataclysmic it would have happened by now. Your scientists know that you are long over-due for such cataclysm but it has not happened. Count your blessings. It is because you deserve to remain for all your growth and your willingness to move back into the Light that you have been given this grace.

From this you will find that your awareness of All That Is begins to grow. You will find that you are feeling different about your life. Perhaps material things will begin to change in importance to you. You will feel a disconnect from things and a calling toward the deeper values of life. Family time may become more important than mall time. Reaching out to others may become more important than putting in more hours at work. Little changes will awaken within you as the energies change in this cycle of time. All of this is leading to the predicted thousands of years of peace. This is how peace is awakened on your planet. This is where you are in this evolutionary cycle. It is a beautiful time to be here. We invite you to explore this more. Be open to the changes that you see bubbling up within yourself and those around you. This is a great time to be on the earth. Enjoy it and be at peace. All is well in the world. The disharmony that you see is made of man. The beauty is also made of man. It is your choice which world you live in.

3:5

HENRIETTA

Let us talk about romance today since we were just discussing the male tree that you met today who referred to himself as George. And so you have the balance between the divine masculine and the divine feminine. Trees do not have gender as such but they are influenced by the elementals that support them and the biological properties of the tree itself. You met a stand of scotch pine today that was not so cordial. That is not only the personality of the tree but the character of the species as well. The scotch pine would be a good stand of trees to have at the perimeter of your property to keep away any wayward creatures that were not there to serve your best interest. Of course a pine tree cannot chase a mangy wolf from your yard but it can emit a scent that would let the wolf know that it was not welcome there. Those in the animal kingdom have much more acute senses than humans and the plant kingdom is known to carry scent. It can be used to attract beneficial insects and deter those which are not beneficial.

I recently watched a documentary about a herd of deer-like animals (I forget the name) living on a reserve in Africa during a drought. There was one tree on the reserve that was able to survive the drought and also was the only source of feed for the herd. In the wild, animals were starving to death because of the lack of vegetation. The herd on the reserve was able to survive only because of the tree that was enduring the drought. Then things turned around and the herd began to die even though they had a source of food. Scientists were called in to investigate. What they discovered was that the tree was producing so many tannins that it was causing the animals to die. The tree, normally safe for consumption, was able to increase the tannins so much that it was enough to kill a large animal! Then, after more research, they discovered that the trees would communicate with each other through a scent that was produced to instruct the neighbouring trees to also increase the tannin production so that they would be protected from the predatory level of consumption of its leaves. The tree, under normal conditions, was safe to consume but when it became the only source of food for the herd and thus was over-consumed, it protected itself with the increased tannins and communicated with its family to do the same!

Back to Henrietta ...

We have led ourselves away from romance. It is an aspect of your existence that is all but lost. It has been replaced by freely given lust. There is no comparison to what the two have to offer. Lust is an empty act of greed whereas romance is a loving dance of desire. Desire is not a bad thing in itself. It is the invitation for creation. It is the instant gratification of one's desires that is creating the discontent in these times. Romance, on the other hand, is the act of holding the fancy of your desire in your thoughts and lovingly creating all that you can to bring your desire into your good graces. It requires the deed of showing one's good character at the hopes of winning the heart of another. Because romance holds one's love near to the heart, anticipating what you will share together, the effects are long-lasting. Romance, or courtship, allows for the anticipation to build, all the time having sweet thoughts of the gem of your desire. When this is missing, the act of coming together does not have the same heart connection and often the results are a feeling of disappointment and emptiness. By moving quickly into the act of communion you give away the sacredness of your union as souls.

There is so much that is lost in this current culture that, if retrieved, would see you living much more joyful lives. What truly matters is dismissed as romantic folly and what does not matter is idolized as truth. You look up to your Hollywood stars, yearning for a life such as theirs.

And yet, if you look closely you will see that most have not found their way to happiness. The answer is not in stardom. The answer is in true love. True love does not idolize. It is more mature than that. It adores but it does not idolize.

And so, what can you take away from this conversation on romance? Many women yearn for it in their lives. It comes alive by seeing the beauty that is you in the eyes of another. It comes from remembering why you were attracted to your loved one. It is to be nurtured like caring for a child. It is the caring of relationships and relationships are a fundamental aspect of being human. So look into your partner's eyes tonight and remember what you love about them. Then create some romance to express your remembering. Magic will happen. If you do not have a partner in your life then dream of romance. Look for it in your choosing of a mate. Hold onto the playfulness that romance brings. When many years have passed and you look back over your life it is the romantic moments that will still be alive in your heart.

Thank you for the opportunity to express this wisdom with you this day Rashana. You are blessed beyond your knowing.

In deep admiration, Henrietta.

3:6

It is another beautiful fall day. The sun is behind clouds but it is warm with a gentle breeze. As I approached the bridge I told Henrietta how much I love the fall. I observed that the chestnut trees seem to be among the first to lose their leaves. She said yes, they give up their leaves to put their energy into developing the fruit that is still clinging to their branches.

As I prepared to sit with Henrietta I gave her a hug and noticed a spot on the bark that looked like a vagina to me. I realized that it is a knot. Several days earlier when I was standing in front of the open part of her trunk I noticed that the knots seemed to go into the core. They are like little sticks going into the center. Today as I observed the knots from the outside and likened them to a vagina Henrietta commented – like a vagina they are connected to the core essence, to the soul you could say. This will make you consider how the vagina should be revered as a connection to the soul. *She asked if I would be interested in discussing that today. Here is a very unexpected conversation to be having with a tree!... OK - any conversation with a tree is unexpected but this one surprised even me!*

First, another warm welcome Rashana. The depth to which you feel love for the Earth these days is a gift to all. Not only to the Earth but to all!

And now we may discuss vaginas. Well not really just vaginas but the spiritual communion that is two people experiencing intercourse. The penetration from one being into another was intended to be a connection to the divine. When you consider that the human heart contains the entire universe you may consider what it means to penetrate the body. When done without love and reverence for What Is then it is like piercing holes in the heart. It is with great sadness that we witness the pain and despair that is created from such wounding. It is used as a weapon by some although we are happy to see that this is changing.

However, even when it is two consenting adults that are engaging in what is lightly called making love, we see that there is no reverence – no sacredness – to the act of uniting in this way. This lack of understanding is wounding many young women and men in your society. It is all taken so lightly that the respect for the act is all but gone. The purpose of this conversation is to have the reader consider how they feel after sexual intercourse that does not include honoring of the person you just merged with. Ask yourself how you truly feel after the moment of passion has passed. If you feel whole and like you have been blessed and you feel closer to the Divine then you have experienced the beauty of this penetration into the heart. If you feel empty and used and lonely then you have pierced your heart instead of filling it with love.

Choose wisely those whom you share your energy with. A piece of their heart stays with you. If it is not a kind and loving heart then you are left resonating in their pain and hardship. This is what we wish you to know and understand. The body is a doorway to the soul. Love yourself and you will attract only love. If you are not fully loving the self then it may be best to refrain from intercourse until you are so that your own soul does not take on more wounding. These are wise words. Many will not see them as such for they do not want to give up their earthly delights. If you only knew the power of these delights when it is a sacred and spiritual connection you would never go back.

Who ever thought that a tree would be talking about sex. But, we say to you that everything contains everything. That is the nature of the hologram you live in. All wisdom is available to you. Maybe someday we will assist you in learning how and where to find it. For now we are delighted to pull from the eternal wisdom that which will support you in your journey.

Remember to notice the trees on your trails. We are the forest through Henrietta.

3:7

GEORGE

Let's talk about wisdom. You see, people think they have wisdom, and many do, but it is the ones who connect with the divine and connect with spirit who are truly wise. It is not the same as intelligence, as many of you know. Wisdom comes from simplicity of being. When you look at all the gurus – Buddha, Jesus, the Dalai Lama, they all live very simple lives. This is where wisdom comes from. One must connect with the stillness within to be fully embraced in the essence of wisdom. This is the way that the plant world lives and therefore you could say that we have wisdom. Our wisdom comes from connecting to the field to retrieve information. We do that as an oversoul that is tree. So, when the human takes time in meditation and sits still and quiets the mind, then they will find wisdom also. They will learn what it is to connect to something other than the self and access knowing from that place. And, in deep meditation, one can be touched by a truth that is the Light of pure love. The physical body would not be able to endure the fullness of that expression of Light, it is too powerful. It can however, access some of the knowing of that wisdom.

This is how trees have an advantage in a way of being able to access this great wisdom. We have no distractions. The winter months are long. The insect world and some of the animal world are all in a state of resting as well and so there is less activity among our branches. We are happy to have the companionship of the birds. We feel them. We recognize their individual characteristics and we delight in their presence. They are a reminder of the activity of life. They are free to soar to heights and so they can rest on any of our branches. As the winter passes, we offer them shelter and a vantage point for their hunting. There is a great symbiosis in the natural world. We do not try to correct it or change it in any way. We flow with it. We accept its intelligence and do not think that we have an intelligence that is above it. Humans do think this way and yet, they do not fully understand the system so they could never beneficially manipulate it. The human way is to take things out of harmony – focusing on one thing or another without the understanding that it is the system as a whole that holds the genius.

When a system is broken down into parts, the genius is lost. This is how you manage your health care system. You break everything down into parts, starting with the human body. Your physicians have not been trained to see the body as a whole system. They break the body down into parts and then they break down the medical profession into specialties that deal with those parts. You have your podiatrists and your gynecologists and your oncologists. None of them see the body as a whole functioning system. When one piece of the system is broken it impacts the whole system but the answer is not to just look at that one symptom. Say it is the liver. The liver breaks down but the cure is not only caring for the liver. What was it that caused the liver to stop functioning fully? What other factors have stressed the liver to have to work so hard? It is all tied together. The same is true for all the natural systems of the world. You cannot take away all the trees and think that the system in which they lived is going to survive. Each piece is part of the whole. The same is true for each person on this earth. Each person has a role to play. The loss of one life does not throw the system out of whack, but it is felt. The same is true when each person sees their worth and understands their role in this world and acts accordingly. The world then runs a little more smoothly. Each piece plays a part. This is my wisdom for today, gathered from the great space that your quantum scientists call 'the field'. Access it yourself and play there for a while. See what there is to discover. I'll meet you there.

I once had an experience that speaks to what George talked about in the beginning of this message when he referred to the Light being too powerful for the physical body to endure. I was interested in Qabala at the time and practicing different meditations to attune to that realm of being. One day while sitting reading Simplified Magic by Ted Andrews I was downloaded with an instant understanding that the potential of what Qabala had to offer was so powerful that it could turn the physical body into dust in a moment. That is to say that I knew that what I was touching into was so powerful that the physical body would not be able to endure the level of energy or 'Light' that it was connected to.

3:8

As an introduction to this message I would like to offer a bit of background. December 21, 2012 was a day that marked the end of an approximately 26,000 year cycle that our solar system passes through. It is called the Precession of the Equinoxes as mentioned earlier. That is what happened on December 21, 2012. It was the end of the Mayan calendar because it was the end of one cycle which also means the beginning of a new cycle. We are now into that new cycle. It is what some call The Age of Aquarius and the predicted thousand years of peace. When you think of the cycle being 26,000 years long, you can understand that it may take a few years to feel the shift from one stage of the cycle to another. However, it is a time to celebrate because we have shifted out of the age of darkness and into the light. This is the cycle that Henrietta is referring to ...

HENRIETTA

You have asked me about humans finding their way back to their true nature and I would say to you that this is something that is changing now that you are at the time of the Precession of the Equinoxes. Everything on the planet and all systems are changing at this time. So to ask of man's true nature, well that is changing as well. People must now rediscover their true nature. We see that there will be a gradual swing back to living closer to the land. People will live in smaller communities, supporting each other with food and skills. This will be a much slower and more enjoyable manner of living than is currently found in your very hectic lifestyles and highly populated community centers. This, in essence, will be finding your way back to your nature as animal. Living closer to the land is a natural state of being for all animal species. Your draw away from the land also led to a disconnect from your true selves. This included your own innate intelligence. As you moved off the land you moved out of your hearts and into the mind. When living in the mind, you lost the connection to the intuitive or more feminine aspect of being and became unbalanced in your importance given to intellectual intelligence. To be intelligent without wisdom is not always useful. It is the wisdom of the intuitive aspect of intelligence that balances what is to be accomplished with that intelligence. There are certain scientists who use their intuition in their work and they are able to make new discoveries at a much higher rate than the more cerebral members of the scientific community.

The intuition is beginning to awaken again on earth and so it too will be leading you back to your true nature regarding your forward progress at this time. It is the intuition that will lead you to natural cures and to the knowing that much has been kept from you. As you awaken to your own inner knowing, many secrets will be revealed, no longer able to be hidden in the energy of awareness that you are awakening into. For this reason, you will begin to manage your energy resources very differently and much will change in this regard. This is good news for your planet, for you almost drove her to extinction. When the oceans are dead the planet and all life upon her are not far behind. We would say that, just in the brink of time, have you found your way back into your hearts so that this destruction of the planet will end. There are genius solutions to all our problems on earth – pollution and such - genius indeed. They will begin to come forward now that the secrets are being revealed and you will quickly be able to heal this planet that has suffered far too long.

So, as a tree, I am delighted to tell you these words and share this understanding. I can see your future as I peer into the All That Is. It is written there, so to speak. Your planet will be saved, with most of the population intact. This makes many happy, for it was the desired outcome. Gaia has protected you more than you know, in order for you to survive. For you see, planets are life forms, just like everything else. All matter comes from Love. All matter. There is no exception. And so it is joyous that Gaia and all her inhabitants are here to live on in this new era. It is this new era that is leading you back to the truth of who you are. You will find more and more that people are open to thinking about the possibility of what they feel when they walk through the forest as opposed to walking through the mall. People will begin to awaken to that as it becomes more spoken of. It is good to be telling people that you speak to a tree. Many will ridicule you, yes. But, you will also give many, many more the permission to be honest about their relationship with trees and all of nature. It has been a bit taboo in your society so it has gone unspoken. The radicals who are willing to step into their truth are the ones that give permission to all. And it is very important now for this to be happening so that you can heal this planet and your very souls along with it. We are delighted to see this happening, for all life everywhere is impacted by what is happening on this planet. You will see in time that this is truth.

3:9

As I sit to connect with Henrietta I see a dragon fly that has landed on a nearby branch of a seedling maple tree. Again I could feel Henrietta connecting with me at my back which is facing her as I sit at her base. Sometimes the love that I feel from her is so real that it touches the depth of my soul. My experience in connecting with trees is that it is a love that is beyond what we normally experience with other humans. It is completely unconditional. The love from Henrietta moves me in the same way as the love from the Ascended Masters and Higher Beings of Light when I channel them. This tells me that the trees are sentinels of this love existing with us here on this earth. It is my greatest joy to be able to awaken humanity to this understanding. It is also my deep hope that we will honor the trees more and appreciate them as sacred sentinels that support our existence in ways that, with this work, we are only beginning to realize.

Henrietta has a very large opening that is about fifteen feet tall up one side of her trunk. It is almost half the width of her trunk. It is also charred, evidence that it has been lit on fire in the past.

"You have a large gap in your trunk that is open. Is this harmful for you?"

And so your question is about my trunk and I say indeed it does affect my well-being – my state of health or wellness you could say. For you see, as my bark separated, it allowed some of my life force to escape. I have healed it as well as I can but, similar to a human scar, the life force can no longer run through that channel. It can disconnect the energy lines which means less than optimal conditions for growth. However, I am a mighty tree with a large trunk and I am able to bring forth enough energy to sustain me. I will be alive on this Earth for many more years.

The following spring I was saddened to see that the large gap in the front of Henrietta had been recently lit on fire. The charred wood filled the entire cavity that travels 15 to 20 feet up her trunk. It then extended up the bark beyond that and onto the adjoining trunk. Since that time I can feel what I would identify as sadness. Henrietta tells me that she is suffering to recover from it. I send healing love every time I am there.

"Is there some wisdom you would like to share?"

Oh yes. I have so much to share. And, again, I am so delighted to have the opportunity to do so. (*The dragon fly is still there on the young maple. Henrietta told me it is recording*). So let us talk about wisdom. This is a time on the Earth unlike any other. It is a time of deep wisdom and grace for those who are leading the way – for those who know what is happening and who are resonating in love. For others it is not so much the case. The wisdom is in living in the moment and knowing that nothing outside of this moment truly matters. There is no need ever to go into the future because it can bring turmoil and fear. But even more, as you realized today Rashana, because it simply does not exist. It is your being in the now and loving what is that allows the beauty of the future to unfold. If you live in the now moment, trusting, then you feel no need to move out of that moment. It is a hard concept for many humans to grasp and yet it is the foundation of living in harmony and joy.

"How can the future not exist if all time exists at once?"

It is as if, by being in the now moment, there is no past or future. By being in the now moment nothing else has any significance what-so-ever. So yes, you could go into your akashic records and see your 'history' there but when you realize the power of now it will not matter to you. Nor will the future. You move into a state of awareness that is only the present moment and you desire nothing else. There is no interest outside of that moment when you reside in this place of existing in the now. It is the place of peace. It is enlightenment. It is the Holy Grail. And we know you feel it. We know it is fully in your awareness. And so you have great wisdom to share Rashana.

"How can people learn to be in the now?"

They must heal. They will have no desire or ability to be there when the wounds are dictating the thoughts. Only those who have the determination, willingness and strength to stay with the emotions and heal them will be rewarded with the peaceful outlook of living in and fully trusting the now moment. You are few although many believe they are there.

As I am writing this it is almost a year since this conversation with Henrietta. I have dedicated the next couple of weeks to finishing this book and putting the conversations together. To start myself off I decided to visit Henrietta for another bit of wisdom. It is interesting what came through today and how it relates to what she shared a year ago. For some reason it moves me emotionally. I think it is because it truly affirms the wisdom that is there by the consistency of the message. Here is what she shared today.

3:10

HENRIETTA

I would like to talk about the times that we are in. Since the beginning of 2013 those who are sensitive are feeling many discordant energies in the world. This is because many are not finding their way in the new reality. They do not understand that the world now works differently and they are struggling.

So many want only love – to be loved – to see love in the world. And yet they do not know that the love must come from within. They project their pain and see it reflected back to them in a continual cycle of hardship, not realizing that it is the lack of self love that is creating the hardship. Those who are sensitive can feel that pain and it creates an energetic field that floats about like radio waves, available to all who have the ability to tune in.

And so it is for those who have found the way back to love of self to balance these energies in the world. By emanating love and joy as much as possible you can greatly assist this evolution. Never before has the earth gone through an evolution like this one. It is profound and it is no wonder that humans are challenged to find their way.

"What can people do to find their way so to speak?"

It is the greatest challenge for humans to be in the moment - to truly be fully present in the now. That is a shame because it is the easiest way to navigate these times. When humans are present in the now they allow life to flow to them. By being fully absorbed in what you are doing as opposed to being fully absorbed in the mind, you will find that you have more joyful moments in your day. However, it is human nature from conditioning, to live more in the mind. This is not so for the few cultures in your world who live fully off the land without modern technology. They are not distracted by the mind with a need for intelligence or to prove their worth. They live by being part of their environment and understanding their connection to the earth and all the creatures of the earth that exist in their environment. This connection to nature keeps them connected to their spirit – their joy. There is no false perception you could say, of what is important. I tell you this so that you may understand that it is culture that has pulled you out of the moment and into the mind. The more one practices living in the moment the more joyful you will be.

Your technology is a great distraction is it not? Do you feel good about yourself at the end of the day after hours of TV? Have you bettered yourself in any way or understood yourself more? We think not. You can change – and many are. It takes the desire as well as the understanding that a change of lifestyle would lead to more contented living. If you do not have that awareness you will not have the desire for change.

"How do people develop that awareness?"

If there is enough discontent then the human is pushed to find another way. For some it must become quite desperate before this will happen. For others it only takes a little trigger, a seed thought, to bring them to contemplate a different awareness – the possibility of a new way of living. This conversation will be that trigger for some.

"Thank you Henrietta. Do you have more wisdom to share today?"

Yes, be love and love yourself first. You cannot love another more than yourself so why not love the self first? Many are unaware of how they do not believe that they deserve love. Explore your relationships and your experiences. They all show you how much love you have for self. If they do not feel loving then forgive yourself and be kind to yourself until you see those relationships begin to change. They will reflect what you truly believe about yourself. There are many books written to help you love the self. That is the basis for this whole discussion. People are lost because they don't love the self enough to welcome a good life.

It is important to note here that there is a difference between wanting and believing. We may want a joyful life full of loving relationships and financial abundance but if we don't believe that we deserve *that life then we will not allow it to come into our experience. I do a lot of work releasing belief systems and it is remarkable how one's life changes once a limiting belief is released. So, when Henrietta talks about welcoming the good life, you may say to yourself that you do that. However, if you don't see it in your reality this would be related to an underlying subconscious belief that causes you to unknowingly resist the very things that you so desire.*

Going back to the beginning of this conversation with Henrietta, when she states that people do not know how to navigate these new energies that we are living in, I know that now, more than ever, our limiting beliefs are creating our reality and it is vitally important to find a way to discover them and release them so that you can create a different reality and indeed allow yourself to receive all the wonderful desires that you can dream of.

Chapter Four

~ Existing in Love ~

> *I frequently tramped eight or ten miles through the deepest snow to keep an appointment with a beech-tree, or a yellow birch, or an old acquaintance among the pines.* *~ Henry David Thoreau ~*

This short chapter speaks to love in a way that many of us never get to experience. It will call you back to self love and it may blow your mind with the huge world of the miniscule that quantum physics is revealing. For eons we have been living in darkness and the suffering has worn us down. We are being called back – called back to our roots. Like the trees anchored into the ground, we are being called back to the origins of creation. As humans existing on this new earth we have a new mandate – to live in love. The greatest need of the hour is the return to love. It is a love like no other that we so deeply yearn for. It is the love of the source from which all life evolves. The trees have offered me a taste of that love. It is so pure and deeply felt that we must heal our wounded past in order to receive it. Only an open heart can taste the love that is offered here.

This love is available to all. There are no favourites in the eyes of All That Is. It only requires willingness and the desire to find one's way back. Our tree friends will help us get there. They are calling out, waiting for us to listen. They have so much to share. Their wisdom continues to reveal deep truth as they offer here about love...

4:1

We the trees see a new world unfolding – a world where love reigns – a world where humans love and support one another. We see a world where humans understand their connection to the Divine through nature. We wait patiently, in strength, as we witness this unfolding.

This is a time of great significance in the evolution of the Earth. Its success requires the open hearts of all who hear these words and the compassionate acts of those who are willing to think outside of the current reality and create a new and beloved Earth. We are here supporting you. Feel us. Hear us call out to you, "Be brave Dear Ones. Be brave." You are all we have, see us, feel us, touch us and find your true nature.

Love is creation. And so you see, as you love deeply you are much more able to recreate your reality. This is a key for the times you are in. It is time to consciously recreate your reality or it will create itself in response to lack of love. That is to say, the more you love the earth and each other, the easier the changes will come and the more beautiful they will be. And so, when we speak of love, we speak of life itself. We speak of existence. We speak of evolution. We speak of the very foundation of life. If love is the foundation of life then the more you are able to receive and give love the more full of life you are. Consider this by thinking of people in your life that you know. Do you find a correlation between those who are loving and the vitality with which they live their lives? There is an important point to be made here. One who is very giving but lives with a victim or martyr mentality is not expressing love. S/he is giving as a need as opposed to being centered in a pure state of love. This is an important discrimination you must make in your review. Love is generous by its mere existence. One who is truly full of love is generous just by being. Those around them can feel it. Indeed some will try to take it – to steal it away – it is so precious.

The power of love can conquer all but it takes a willing heart, one that has recognized that love brings life and is the true place of power. Evil has no power over love. If you only knew that you would laugh at the folly that you have lived, letting fear hold you back for so long. This is a reason to love the self – to step into your power of being love and standing strong in the light of love like a warrior for Spirit. Strong are they who feel so much love from the Divine that they are invincible. They are invincible not because the physical body cannot be harmed but because the Spirit cannot be harmed.

4:2

All this talk about love has a deep purpose. If we are to create the life of our dreams we have to first believe that we deserve it. In my work facilitating my own healing and guiding others to the same I have learned that we create from our beliefs. If we are not fully loving the self, we will not believe that we deserve the life we desire and therefore will not allow it into our life expression. Most often the beliefs that limit our dreams are hidden in the subconscious. It is for that reason that, by finding our way back to self love, we will then allow a new expression of life. Henrietta speaks of it in the following message where she asked me the question for a change.

I would like to share about love. What do you think love is? ***"It is the unconditional appreciation for all life."*** That is a very good answer. It surprises me actually. You have a good grasp of what love is. So, we will use your words to speak of love. First you used the word unconditional. That is an important aspect of real love. There are no conditions. You do not have to behave a certain way or meet any expectations of another. Real love accepts ALL that is. So, that is a good word to use to start the definition. Then you speak of appreciation - again, a very wise choice. Appreciation does not speak of neediness, which is what many humans equate love with. Appreciation also has no conditions. When one is in appreciation for all life, then there is regard for all life. If you are appreciating something, you cannot be critical of it. So, if humans could find the place of appreciating everything and everyone, the world would be full of love.

What else could we say of love? ***"We could say that it is acceptance."*** Yes indeed. Acceptance is another aspect of love. This is the key to self love, which is where all love comes from. If you accept all aspects of who you are then you will be loving yourself. When you are loving yourself, there is no need to criticize or belittle yourself or others. So acceptance means allowing. You allow yourself to be who you are and you allow others to be who they are as well. We now have in our definition the words appreciation, acceptance and allowing. The three As of love. We would like you to remember this and use it for positive self regard. For you see, love is the foundation to happiness. It does not come from another. It does not come from possessions. It does not come from accomplishments. It comes from the appreciation and acceptance of the self. And when you are in appreciation and acceptance of the self, then you allow the self to express honestly in the world. There is no need to put on a face of what the world wants to see. There is no need to try to be someone else, believing that you are less than perfect. There is no need to try and fit a mold. You are the mold of you. It is when you try to fit into another's perception of what your mold should be that you suffer. End the suffering by accepting that you are perfect just the way you are. Maybe you do not always behave in ways that you like, but when you start truly accepting and appreciation yourself, you will stop behaving in that way. The more you love yourself the less unlovable you become, based on society's interpretations of love. The more you love yourself, the less you have to act out - crying out for love. You have it within.

Searching for love outside of the self is never successful. Others will always view you from their perspective and their expectations, unless they are in the three As of love themselves. Then they will see you as perfect and will not look to you to fill their empty heart space. If they are not searching outside of themselves, then they will not look to you for their awareness of love. But, if you are searching for love outside of yourself with others who are doing the same, that is the formula for suffering. They will not see the fullness of you. They cannot because they do not see it for themselves. Therefore they will expect you to fill the emptiness that they experience and when you do not live up to those expectations, the honeymoon is over. Whereas, when your love comes from within, there is no honeymoon period. It is balanced love. It is not the highs and lows of emotion. It is the deep seated feeling state of love. There is a difference. Only those who get glimpses of the depth of unconditional love have an awareness of what that truly feels like.

The world has and is still changing. In order for humanity to keep up with the evolution of the earth, there is the need to find this love within the self. Without it, people will be living the expression of not love. And that does not feel very good. We are in a new time with new energies on the earth. Those energies mean that more than ever man is a creator of his own life. What you create is a reflection of your love of self and what you believe you deserve.

4:3

In contrast to that simple yet profound message from Henrietta, the following message from George takes a huge leap into a much deeper awareness of existence. He offers a glimpse into discoveries that are just emerging from the field of quantum physics. I include it here to ignite a spark in your awareness, perhaps triggering a deeper knowing that rests within your psyche. There is a part of our being – our soul – that knows all.

Trees have an overview of all life. We stand as sentinels of the physical world and yet we also are connected to all life everywhere. We know the birds and the bugs and the wind and the rain. We know it. We don't just endure it – we know it. This is something that humans can be at one with as well, but you are not. You have been lost for so long that you have forgotten. To 'know' these things is to be a part of their essence. I stand as tree and yet I know that I am not tree. I am particles come together to represent tree. And bird is particles come together to represent bird. And wind is …. You get it. With this knowing, I do not identify with tree as such, but with All That Is. I am not tree, I am all That Is presenting as tree. This is confusing for some, for many of you do not have the understanding of how life is created. You are moving into times when many are telling you that life is what you create. This is what we are referring to here. Knowing that you create with your mind will help you understand what I am saying. If you cannot connect with the reality of that awareness, it is hard for you to understand what I speak of.

To grasp what I am saying, allow yourself to imagine that everything in your awareness is an interpretation, which it is. It is a visual that goes through the eyes, is then interpreted by the mind and becomes an understanding from there. It is your awareness, your perspective that creates your life. One person can experience a movie and come out with a totally different feeling from someone else who just watched the same movie. It triggers different emotions and pulls on different belief systems for each person. In this way, each is creating their own experience.

This is what we would like you to understand. Your experience is made up of your internal systems of thought and beliefs. If you believe that life supports you and that mostly good things happen to you, that is what you will create in your experience. What you create out of the particles that quantum physics calls the field, is good experiences. Another person could be standing beside you or driving behind you and believe that life is hardship and nothing goes right and have a totally different experience. This is just another way to say that the human experience comes from thought. The human believes that s/he is separate from all life and does not see that the field is all life. S/he has the experience of being a thing – a human that believes it is separate from the rest of creation - whereas a tree knows that it is not a thing, it is just the particles of all life coming together to appear as a thing. It appears as a thing because a human believes it is such. What the human believes the mind will create for the human to see. A tree presents as tree but does not solely identify as tree. It identifies as All That Is presenting as tree.

Place your hand on a tree and the separation will not be so strong. You will feel the connection. You will feel the tree sharing itself – its particles – with you, if you are open to such a feeling. If you do not believe it is possible then you will not feel it because, again, you are creating your world. We are expanding your mind here. This is our experience as tree. It is why we can emanate so much love into the world. It is why we can be cut down en masse and not have hatred or regret. We are love particles come together to give you the experience of tree and we 'love' to send our energy to you. We see and know that humans need love and so we offer it to you. If you believe that love is your experience then you will say yes to it and receive it. We will be happy then, for we will have fulfilled our intention which is love. The particle field in which all matter comes to life is nothing but love.

Part III

~ Back to Our Roots ~

Sometimes Thou may'st walk in Groves, which being full of Majestie will much advance the Soul.
~ Thomas Vaughan ~

I am writing this book at a time when the earth is being raped and pillaged at an alarming rate. Forests are being burned and clear cut, foods are being genetically manipulated, wild animals are moving into cities and people are getting sick and depressed. The skies are being sprayed with chemicals and the oceans are being filled with plastic. If I wasn't such an optimist I would say that things are a mess. It would appear that the entire ecosystem of our planet is on the brink of destruction, and I believe I know what got us here. We are disconnected from nature. Just look at the lives of our children. They run from school, to after school programs then home for a quick bite to eat before running out again for other extra-curricular activities. In between they are watching TV, playing video games or texting. Most kids are doing anything but playing freely in the great outdoors. When they do go out to play it is to a playground or a park where the environment is controlled and the children are corralled to safe areas under the watchful eyes of their caregivers. What is lost is the freedom to run and explore, to discover and be pulled into the wonder of nature.

The more disconnected from nature we are the less happiness we have in our lives. Studies have shown that people living in some of the poorest countries of the world have more happiness than we do in the western world. We have all the stuff and they, living closer to the land with less stuff, have more joy! Why would this be? We have been taught to think that the more we have the happier we will be. The more technology we have the better life becomes. And yet, if you stop and reflect, you may find that you are not really very happy at all. The truth is that most people are searching for joy by wishing for things and yearning for more yet never truly satisfied.

Could it be that by connecting more with the natural world we will connect more with ourselves and each other? I believe so. I believe that it is our disconnect from nature that has us so sick and unhappy. I also believe that it is that disconnection that has allowed us to take from the earth without ever thinking of giving back or maintaining the incredibly complicated and intelligent ecosystems of the natural world.

There is a grand intelligence at work in nature. Just look at a flower and consider that it started as a seed and grew into a plant and bloomed and gave off a pleasing aroma. What is it that allowed all that to happen? Oh yes, we know that the seed lies dormant and then rain and sunshine coax it to life. But, what is the potential there that knows what is to happen with the moist rain and warm sunshine? It is the same intelligence that created us humans. It is the same intelligence that allows us to breathe and have thoughts. I call that intelligence soul or love. It is in you. It is in me. And, to some degree, it is in everything in nature. That is why it is vital that we find our way back. As we appreciate nature we learn to appreciate our true essence. We return to our souls and we find true joy and happiness. That, I believe, is why the cultures that live close to the land, with few possessions, can be happier than those in the western world. They know something we don't. They know that our stuff is not going to make us happy. It is our connection to nature, to our souls and each other, where we will find fulfillment.

~ A final message ~

Thank you for joining me on this journey to discover the profound wisdom and love that has been waiting for us in the natural realms of existence. Because I believe that it is possible to communicate intuitively with trees, I am able to collect this wisdom. It is a skill that we all possess. I do not have magical powers. What I do have is a desire to know life from a greater perspective than the logical mind perceives and a belief that anything is possible. Through the process of noticing the trees and the desire for a deeper connection I send love, appreciation and gratitude to the trees for their existence. In return, I feel their love and sense, know or hear their wisdom. You can do this too. You can connect to a tree by greeting it with an open heart, sending love and appreciation for its beauty and its being. You can ask the tree what it would like to share with you and listen with your heart for the answer. You can lean against the trunk of a tree and ask it to take away all your worries and concerns. You can ask it to energize you and make you well. With an open heart and practice you can access this wisdom for yourself.

This book was written for those of you who are ready to live in a new world – a world where humans are connecting heart to heart. It is written to awaken the desire for a world where we remember our connection to the land and we honor all of creation. It is written to create a new potential on the earth – one created from love. We are magnificent Beings awakening. Open your eyes to the potential for change. Turn your gaze away from the limitations of the past. We can create heaven on earth.

The way back is not complicated. It is only the mind that wants to make it so. When we invite our heart into our knowing we develop wisdom. Such wisdom is so eloquently spoken by George that I offer it here as the final word. May it rest upon your heart as a gentle invitation home ~ home to our roots, the very origin of life ...

"What can a tree tell humans about love?"

We can tell you what true love feels like. There is no judgement – ever! Love does not judge, it accepts. A tree knows that love because it does not have the mind that creates scenarios that are out of harmony with the truth. A tree knows love as the essence of life – the light from the sun and the nourishment from the earth. The mere sustenance of life is a gift of love. Knowing that everything we need to survive is provided to us is love.

This is true for humans as well but you have lost that understanding. You have forgotten that all your needs are provided for. You have forgotten to appreciate the sun for the life it brings and to thank your earthly mother for the land beneath your feet. You have forgotten that the song birds sing for your delight. You have forgotten that the flowers bloom to appeal to your senses. We, the trees, have not forgotten, for it is all we have. We are not distracted by the need for creation other than growing and sustaining ourselves. Therefore, we do not see anything but what is. Sometimes we see love in people and sometimes we see fear covering up that love.

Trees are kind to one another. We will grow where we are planted. If two seedlings start life side by side they share the soil and the sunlight and they may grow into tall, stately trees, side by side, sharing and existing together. Do they feel each other? Oh yes. They do and they come to appreciate their existence in that way. They learn to live harmoniously. When they have completed their cycle on the earth and one falls, it may take the other down with it. There will be nothing but total acceptance of that. There are no conditions of existence as a tree, other than the environment. Love is easy for a tree. As the trees take their sustenance from the earth and the sky, they also draw prana from the ethers and they offer it back to the earth. This is love. Prana is love. Chi, energy, it is all love. The very force that keeps you alive is love. Have you thought of it that way? It is nothing less than love. So the mere fact that you are here walking the earth is love. You are so removed from that now that you have forgotten. I am happy to remind you, for this realization can change your life if you allow it. If you give it enough of your attention you will be changed. You breathe love. You walk love. You exist – love in action. That is what you are at the core.

How you think you could live without love is merely a reflection of your forgetting. As you go about your day remember that the energy that keeps you moving is love. As you breathe remember that you are breathing love. And where did that air come from? It has passed through the trunks of trees. It has moved through the lungs of lovers as they join in passionate joy. It has nourished a newborn babe taking its first breath. This is the wonder of life. It is all shared. You are not alone. You have breathed the breath of someone on the other side of the world. Is this not love? It is beautiful. It is delight. It is joy. It is heaven. That of which I speak is heaven on earth. All you have to do is remember and hold it in your awareness and you will create heaven on earth once again. It is so simple.

Humans like to complicate things, but it is so simple. Love is all there is.

About the Author

Rashana lives in the beautiful province of Nova Scotia, Canada. She is an Intuitive Counselor, Channeler, Reiki Master, Certified Hypnotherapist, Sound Healer, the Creator of Rashana Sound Essences and The Freedom Release Technique.

Rashana has appeared on national television, several radio shows and in front of large audiences. She has recorded 2 CDs and just completed her sixth book. Learn more at www.rashana.ca

29858231R10094

Made in the USA
Charleston, SC
27 May 2014